1

Scientific and Esoteric Encyclopedia of UFOs, Aliens and Extraterrestrial Gods

Volume V: A (Anunnaki-Ayling)
From a set of 20 volumes.
*** *** ***

Maximillien de Lafayette

Volume V

SCIENTIFIC AND ESOTERIC ENCYCLOPEDIA OF UFOS, ALIENS AND EXTRATERRESTRIAL GODS

The world's first and most authoritative encyclopedia of its kind!!

Published in the United States of America and Germany.

Printed by Times Square Press. New York.
Date of Publication: July 20, 2014.

Scientific and Esoteric Encyclopedia of UFOs, Aliens and Extraterrestrial Gods

Volume V: A (Anunnaki-Ayling) from a set of 20 volumes.

Maximillien de Lafayette

*** *** ***

Times Square Press
New York   Berlin   Paris   Madrid
2014

Table Of Contents

9

Table of contents

- What the aliens or extraterrestrials would not do.
- What the aliens or extraterrestrials would or could do.
- Should the German New World Order UFOs and their scientists decide to attack us.
- Project Omega.
- The Grays, General Marshall, President Eisenhower, and D-Day.
- The device used to create a holographic projection.
- HZ: An acronym for Holographic Zooming.
- The New Wonder-Weapons of the Nazi New World Order.
- No country on Earth is safe from this apocalyptic annihilation except.
- Au, Aw, Awu.
- Aurora airship crash in Texas, April 17, 1897, the.
- AUTEC (Atlantic Undersea Test and Evaluation Center).
- Sophisticated and Exotic Aliens' Weapons Systems at AUTEC.
- Weapons systems out of this world.
- HZP: An acronym for Holographic Zooming Project.
- Earth-made holographic zooming.
- Extraterrestrials-made holographic zooming.
- Holographic zooming going on at some intelligence agencies.
- Statement from Northrop Grumman.
- D.S.I (Deep Sea Integrated Bubbles Program).
- D. S. I. and the extraterrestrials.
- AUTEC and the Atlantis scenario.
- AUTEC underwater military bases.
- The "Spinning Mobile Satellite".
- Authors, thinkers, scientists, investigators, witnesses, dignitaries, and personalities who made an impact on ufology.
- Autopsy of an aliens' dead body.
- Aviary.
- Avikhal "Abi-Khal".

- AVRO.
- Aya.
- Ayling.

*** *** ***

A

Continued from Volume IV.

Anunnaki chronology.

Luxor, previously known as Thebes.

Inscription on a brick from the Tower of Babel.
Blockprint, Babylon, 604-562, Babylon.
Some historians have associated the Temple of Marduk with the
Tower of Babel. This association was never documented or
substantiated.

3,000 B.C.: The Hayasa-Azzi tribes first inhabit Urartu.
2,900 B.C.: Erech becomes King of Sumer.
Inanna rules over the Third Region known as the Indus Valley.

2,650 B.C.: Mutiny in the kingdom of Sumer.
The Anunnaki's king, Enlil is disappointed by the behavior of the human race.
2,500 B.C.: Two Assyrian cities Arbel and Nineveh prosper and their trade flourishes in the Near East.
2,371 B.C.: Sargon erects Agade, the new capital of the mighty empire of Akkad.
2,316 B.C.: Sargon's power is unchallenged in Babylon.
Marduk fights Inanna.
Marduk leaves Mesopotamia.
2,300 B.C.: The power of the Sumerians had declined to such an extent that they could no longer defend themselves against foreign invasion.
2,291 B.C.: Naram-Sin ascends the throne of Akkad.
Aided by Inanna, he occupies the Sinai Peninsula, and captures Egypt.
2,255 B.C.: The Anunnaki destroy Agade.
Inanna seizes power in Mesopotamia, but her reign would not last long after the defeat of Nippur on the hands of Naram-Sin.
The allied armies of Ninurta and Enlil invade and occupy Akkad and Sumer.
2,220 B.C.: Sumerian civilization reaches its peak.
The legendary Ziggurat temple in honor of Ninurta is erected by king Gudea.
New laws and ethics code are established by the rulers of Lagash.
2,200 B.C.: Amorites invaded Phoenicia.
2,193 B.C.: Terah, Abraham's father is born in the city of Nippur to a prominent priestly-royal family.
2,180 B.C.: The kingdom of Egypt is divided;
Ra-Marduk subjects remained in the south.
Pharaohs retained Lower Egypt.
2,150 B.C.: The Anunnaki left earth for good.
They paid a short visit to Phoenicia, and the Island of Arwad.
2,130 B.C.: Inanna's last attempt to regain her throne.
2,123 B.C.: Abraham is born in Nippur.
2,100 B.C.:
Discovery of the "ORME" invented by Tubaal Kain (Tubal-Caiin). Only members of the royal family and the first hierarchy of Sumerian priesthood had access to it.

Naram-Sin king of Akkad on his victory stele. 23rd century B.C. Aided by Inanna, he occupies the Sinai Peninsula, and captures Egypt.

King Gudea.

19

Sargon on a bas-relief from Khorsabad.

The walls of Nineveh.

In common term, it was called "Man-nah-Iyil", the "Elixir of Eternal Life." But this formula was not successful. Originally created to replace the lost "Orme", the "Man-nah-Iyil", was later used in alchemy. Centuries later, it will be known to medieval alchemists as the "Philosophical Stone."

The French Ulema and alchemist Nicholas Flammel allegedly deciphered a part of its code, and succeeded in transmuting metal into pure gold.

Many French historians attribute his sudden wealth to his discovery of the "Philosophical Stone."

21

The medieval Philosophical Stone.

Nicholas Flamel

Nicholas Flammel, circa 1416.

2,096 B.C.: Ur-Nammu is defeated.

He died from severe injuries on the battlefield.

His military commanders are dispersed and his army is totally annihilated. This year marked the departure of Terah to Harran.

2,095 B.C.: Shulgi became the king of Ur.

2,090 B.C.: A major part of the highly advanced Anunnaki technology and science is lost.

The human race was not prepared or ready to fully understand how the Anunnaki's advanced tools functioned.

2,080 B.C.: Nabu, the son of Marduk gains major influence in Western Asia.

2,070 B.C.: Marduk, king of mighty Babylonia is the last royal remnant of the Anunnaki on earth. Marduk is worshiped as god.

2,065 B.C.: Enlil is no longer controlling the human race.

2,060 B.C.: Abraham left Ur and headed toward Harran.

2,055 B.C.: Revolt in major Canaanite cities.

23

Mud houses at Harran.
In 2,060 B.C., Abraham left Ur and headed toward Harran.

The Elamite troops crashed the revolt and restored order.

2,050 B.C.: Marked the beginning of the decline of the Sumerian civilization, caused in part by the departure of the Anunnaki.

2,048 B.C.: Shulgi died.

Leading five legions of warriors, AV-raham (The early one) captured the lands of Canaan.

2,047 B.C.: Amar-Sin (the Biblical Amraphel) becomes king of Ur. Avraham is defeated. He retreats to Egypt, stays there five years, and then returns with more military legions.

2,041 B.C.: Guided by Inanna, Amar-Sin creates a formidable military coalition with the Kings of the East, and attacks the lands of Canaan and Sinai. But Avraham interferes and his blocks Amar-Sin at the main entrance of the "Space port."

Note: Two separate Abrahams existed in history; Avraham was a warrior, the other is the Biblical Patriarch.

The ruins of Harran, the homeland of Abraham.

2,038 B.C.: Shu-Sin replaces Amar-Sin on throne of Ur.

2,029 B.C.: Ibbi-Sin replaces Shu-Si Marduk gains popularity.

2,024 B.C.: Leading a might army Marduk marches on Sumer, captures the city and declares himself king. Enlil is furious and demands that Marduk and Nabu be punished; Enki sides with Marduk, but his son Nergal sides with Enlil.

2,113 B.C.: Nammmu reigns over Nippur.

Enlil appoints Nannar, lord of Shem. T
he city of Ur became the capital of the Anunnaki's empire.

1,800 B.C.: The Hyksos invaded Phoenicia.

1,760 B.C.: Hammurabi king of Babylonia conquers Assyria and put an end to the first Assyrian empire.

1,500 B.C., Egypt: The Palace of Pharaoh Thutmosis III.
Many circles of raging fire are said to have hovered over the royal palace while fishes, winged creatures, and other objects rained down from the sky.

1,363 B.C.: Mitanni rules Assyria with an iron hand.

1,362-64 B.C.:
The Phoenicians became the first civilization to capture the sounds of words in writing by inventing the alphabet; a writing system consisting of individual letters. Several letters were taken from the Anakh (Anunnaki) language.

Sumerian cuneiforms (wedge shaped symbols in clay tablets) and Egyptian hieroglyphics (pictographs) were the only known forms of writing before the Phoenician alphabet. Both scripts, though separately created, used picture writing.
Eventually, pictures or signs represented sounds, and finally, the pictures and signs became so simplified that a whole word was written as a single sign. The Phoenicians developed symbols which in time became a real alphabet.
The Phoenician alphabet consisted of twenty-two symbols, all consonants.

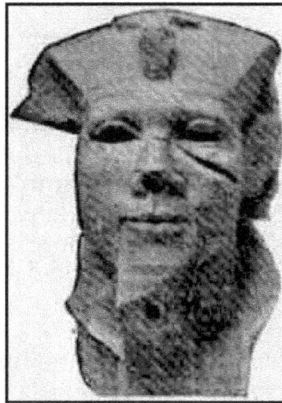

Apepa, King of the Hyksos.

26

The stele of Ur-Nammu, circa 2200 B.C.

A group of Phoenicians from the early days of Tyre and Sidon.
The early Phoenicians who lived in Arwad were the descendants
of the remnants of the Anunnaki who landed on Earth some
450,000 years ago.

Each one represented its own sound.

The Egyptian symbol for the Ox-head was given the Semitic name aleph, and was sounded as "a." The symbol for house became Beth, and was sounded as "b."

Egyptians texts made references to the advanced scientific technology found in the cities of Tyre, Sidon, Byblos, Beirut and Zaraphath.

1,260 B.C.: The Assyrians scribes and inscriptions mention Urartu for the first time.

1,240 B.C.: Babylon is ravaged by the Assyrians.

1,200 B.C.: The Assyrians resist incursions by the Urarturians and the Mushki.

1,155 B.C.: Elam and Assyria attack Babylonia and put an end to the Kassite rule.

1,114 to 1,076 B.C.: This era marked the reign of Tiglath-Pileser the first over Assyria.

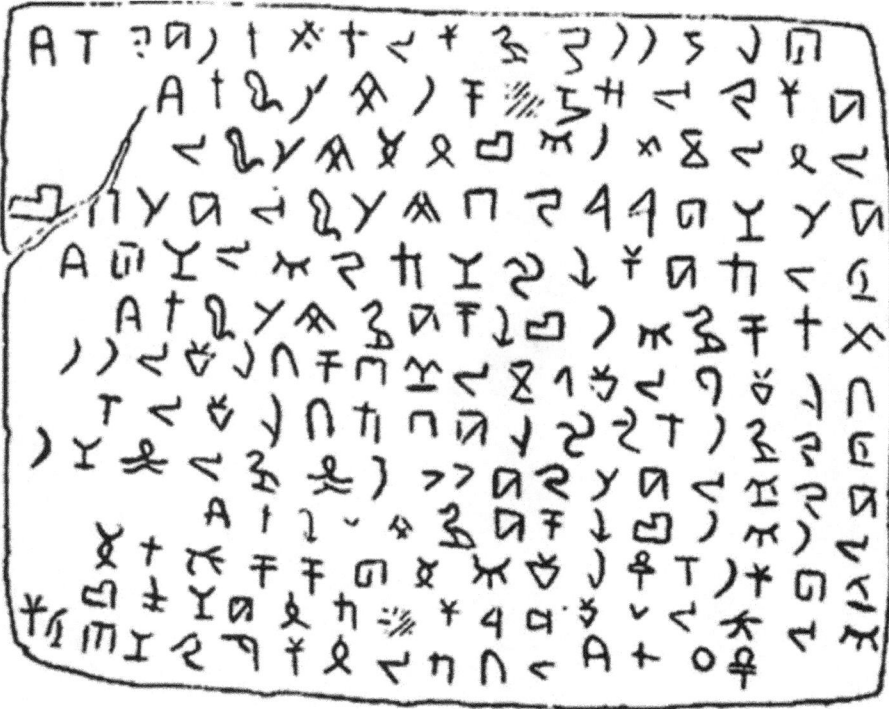

Byblos script.

Byblos (Jbeil) was an ancient, prosperous and influential Phoenician city along the coast of modern day Lebanon. According to several linguists, its name was the origin of the Greek word "biblio" which means book. Others have said it was vice versa, or just the opposite.

Bas-relief of Tiglath-Pileser, from the Central Palace at
Nimrud.

Royal inscription of Naram-sîn: Naram-sîn, builder of the temple of Inanna. Clay, Akkad, Sumer, 2291-2254 B.C., a brick printing block, with a large loop handle. Only two brick printing blocks of Naram-Sîn known, were found in Iraq. One with a cylindrical handle in Istanbul, Turkey, the other is on display at the British Museum. Naram-Sîn was the first Babylonian king to use blocks for printing.

1,080 B.C.: Egyptian story of Wen-Amen, mentioned Wereket-El, a Phoenician ships builder who lived in Tanis in the Nile delta. Reference was made to the triangle insignia he placed on his ships. In ancient times, the "triangle" was the logo of the Anunnaki who landed in Phoenicia.

1,000 B.C.:
Major historical events happened that year:
1-The Phyrgians and the Thracians immigrate to Urartu.
2-The Phoenician city Tyre established colonies throughout the Mediterranean areas and strengthened its commercial ties with the Hyksos (Anunnaki descendants) in Cilicia.
Zinjirli ruled by King Kilamuwa, a remnant of the Anunnaki.
King Kilamuwa adopted the Phoenician language that contained Anunnaki's letters and symbols.
Anunnaki's and Phoenicians scripts were engraved at the main entrance of the royal palace in Ancient Armenia.

Bronze plate of Balawat representing the campaign of Salamanzar the third against Urartu.

Map of Cilicia.

MAP of ARMENIAn KINGDOM of CILICIA

3- Hiram, the Phoenician king of Tyre, became the military ally and business partner of King Solomon. Expedition "Ophir" was carried out by King Solomon and King Hiram.

Legend has it that Phoenician ships sailing the Mediterranean were guided by a mysterious light in the form of a crescent hovering over their ships.

4-The Urarturians conquer and overrun the majority of the lands of the mighty empire of Assyria. In exchange for peace, the Phoenicians shared with the Urarturians secret knowledge they have acquired from the Anunnaki; this included maritime compasses and celestial maps and arithmetic formula written in Ana'kh (Anunnaki language.)

At that time in history, the Phoenicians referred to the Anunnaki as Anakh.

5-In Tyre/Sidon cities, the Phoenicians discovered "Ourjouwan"; the famous dye known as the "Tyrian Purple".

Ancient Mesopotamian and Phoenicians tablets mentioned this dye as the "heavenly color" of the Anakh (Anunnaki).

33

332 B.C.-64 B.C.:
Phoenicia fades away:
Phoenicia faded away with the destruction of its major city Tyre on the hands of the unmerciful and vengeful Alexander of Macedonia.
Phoenicia was totally absorbed by the Greeks, and the magnificent historical Phoenician identity vanished for ever. When Alexander of Macedonia invaded Asia and defeated the Persian Empire in 333 B.C., Sidon, (Saida), the Island of Arwad (Road), and Byblos (Jbeil) were absorbed by Macedonia.
Tyre, the most important Phoenician city resisted Alexander and refused to allow him to enter the temple of its supreme god. This infuriated Alexander.

Ruins of Tushpa-van, the capital of kingdom of Urartu. The early Urarturians were the remnants of Anunnaki offspring.

Thus, Alexander decided to destroy Tyre. However, it took him a 7-month siege in 332 B.C. to capture the city. After its bloody defeat, Tyre was reduced to ashes, and the Phoenicians gradually lost their national identity.
The whole country became part of Alexander's Greco-Macedonian empire.
In 64 B.C., the name of Phoenicia disappeared from history, when its lands were made part of the Roman province of Syria.

Phoenicians of Tyre, from a Persepolis relief, 5th century, B.C.

The army of Alexander entering the old city of Tyre.

Siege of Tyre by Alexander the Great.

A Phoenician prince bring gifts to King Solomon.
An envoy of King Hiram of Tyre, brining gifts to King Solomon. Hiram was the primordial founder of the freemasonry, and custodian of many of the Anunnaki-Ulema scrolls. Hiram was also a close friend and ally of King Solomon. Hiram's daughter was one of the wives of Solomon.

It was this Phoenician princess who introduced the Phoenician religion and god El "Baal" to the Israelites.

Later on, the prophets of Israel would wage wars against Baal and El, (Who were the prototypes of their own god Yahweh), because they felt that Judaism was seriously threatened by the cult of Baal.

Anunnaki's Kiriba:
I. Definition and introduction
II. From Sumer, we have
II. From Sumer, we have
III. From Babylon, we have
IV. From Akkad, we have
V. From the kings of Isin, we have
VI. From the Dynasty of Amurru, we have
VII. From the Dynasty of Kassites, we have
VIII. From the Chaldean Dynasty, we have

I. Definition and introduction:

A genealogy line of the descendants and/or remnants of the Anunnaki's remnants on Earth, in the regions of Mesopotamia, Babylonia, Sumer, Assyria, Chaldea, Phoenicia, and Turkey.

It is also a register of names in a chronological order.

The Book of Ramadosh listed all the names and assumed functions of these individuals. In addition to an elaborate list of mythological figures, the list included monarchs and leaders who played a significant role in the establishment and development of dynasties and civilizations in the Near and Middle East, such as Assur-Nasir Pal (Aššurnasirpal) of Assyria, Sargon, Šamši-Adad, several kings of Elam, starting with the Avan and Simash dynasties, and ending with the Babylonian and Shuttrukid dynasties.

The list also includes some of the kings of Mari, like Il'Shu, and Ikun-Ishtar. And of course, several kings of Sumer.

II. From Sumer, we have:

- 1- Alulim, who ruled for 28,800 years.
- 2- Alalgar, who ruled for 36,000 years.
- 3- Enmen-gal-ana, who ruled for 28,800 years.
- 4- Dumuzi, who ruled for 36,000 years.
- 5- En-sipad-zid-ana, who ruled for 28,800 years.
- 6- Ubara-Tutu, who ruled for 18,600.

Aššurnasirpal

Stone panel from the Palace of Ashurnasirpal II, Nimrud, circa 883-859 B.C.

Stone panel from the Palace of Ashurnasirpal II, 883-859 B.C.

A slab depicting musicians and attendants of Ashurbanipal.

III. From Babylon, we have:

The register includes some of the kings of Babylon, before the Great Flood.

* 1- Alulim, who reigned in Eridu.
* 2- Enmenlu'anna, who reigned in Badgurgurru.
* 3- Sibzianna, who reigned in Larak.
* 4- Utnapishtim (Xinsuddu), who reigned in Shurruppak.
* 5- Nimrud, founder of Bab-El (The gate of God), then re-named Bab-Ilani (The Gate of Elohim), who was the first Sumerian king. After he built the Tower of Babel, the kingdom lost unity and Sumerian cities became self-ruled "State-Cities".

Note: The Sumerian states collapsed with the expansion of Semitic peoples, and the Akkadian kings took control over the lower Mesopotamia. The first Akkadian king mentioned is the same as the first
Assyrian king, Sharyukenu, known in history as Sargon, is to be identified with the Biblical Ashur (Assur), founder of the Assyrian state.

IV. From Akkad, we have:

* 1- Sharyukenu (Sargon I)
* 2- Rimush
* 3- Manishtushu
* 4- Naramsu'in/Naram-sin
* 5- Sharkalisharri
* 6- Elulu'mesh
* 7- Dud'u
* 8- Shu'durul

V. From the kings of Isin, we have:

* Ishbi'erra, in Naplanum.
* 2- Shu'ilishu, in Ymisium.
* 3- Ishmedagan, in Zabaya.
* 4- Enlilbani, in Sineribam.

VI. From the Dynasty of Amurru, we have:

* 1- Nimrod

- 2- Sumuabum
- 3- Sumula'el

King Sargon (Sharru-Kin) from Nineveh.

Stele of Sargon's slaves.

- 4- Sabium
- 5- Aplisin
- 6- Sinmuballit
- 7- Hammurabi

VII. From the Dynasty of Kassites, we have:
- 1- Gandash
- 2- Akum
- 3- Kashtiliash
- 4- Ushshi
- 5- Abirattash
- 6- Urzigurumash

VIII. From the Chaldean Dynasty, we have:
- 1- Simmashshikhu
- 2- Eamukhinshumi
- 3- Kashshunadin

- 4- Eulmashshakinshumi
- 5- Ninurta'kudurrussur
- 6- Shiriqtishukamunu
- 7- Marbiti'apalussur
- 8- Nabumukinapli
- 9- Shamashmudammiq
- 10- Nabushumishkun
- 11- Mardukzakirshumi
- 12- Mardukbalatzuiqbi

Anunnaki Ulema: Daraja is the name of the Anunnaki Ulema categories and classes, which are:
- **a**-The Noubahari "Noubarim", "Noubari", "Noubaha';
- **b**-The Mou-Na.rin "Mounawariin", "M'Noura-Iin";
- **c**-The Gayir-Mirayin "Gayrmirayim";
- **d**-The Ari-Siin "Arishim".

The Anunnaki Ulema are classified and categorized as follows, by order of importance and hierarchy, starting from the lowest level to the highest one:

1-Category One:
The Noubahari, "Noubarim", "Noubari".
Noubahari is the plural of Noubih.
Noubih is either a noun or an adjective. It means alert, informed, observant, wise, messenger of truth and wisdom.
From Noubih, derived the Sumerian and Akkadian words Nabih or Na. Bih, which means messenger, and the Arabic word Nabih, which means wise, intelligent, and well- informed.
The Noubahari are humans, and they live on earth. Physically, they are not very much different from the rest of us. But on other levels, they are far more superior.

For instance (to name a few):
- **1**-They do not age as rapidly as we do. A seventy year old Ulema looks like a 37 year old man. Ulema Sadik said: "Physically, the Ulema do not look older then 37...and they stay like that for the rest of their lives..."
- **2**-Ulema live longer than ordinary human beings. Their lifespan on earth is approximately 135 years.

46

- **3**-They are vegetarians.
- Yes, they do drink, but with moderation. Some smoke, but not cigarettes. Their tobacco is made out of aromatic dried fruits.
- **4**-They have an enormous compassion toward animals. They communicate exceptionally well with animals; the majority of animals except crocodiles, snakes, insects carrying bacteria and diseases, and some reptiles species. Animals sense their presence and welcome them.
- Ulema have developed a sign language to facilitate their communication with animals. And usually, animals respond in the same manner.
- **5**-Ulema are well-versed in many languages. And they are fond of languages of ancient civilizations, including those of vanished cultures. Ulema learn foreign languages very easily and rapidly. Usually, an Ulema learns a foreign language in less than a week.
- **6**-Ulema can read a voluminous book and memorize it in its entirety in less than three hours.
- **7**-Ulema can foresee the future and predict events to happen in several dimensions, including our own.
- **8**-Ulema are in constant contact with the Guardians.
- **9**-Ulema knowledge in arts, science, history and religions is limitless, etc...

These qualities and gifts allow them to fully understand the human psyche, read our minds, and sympathize with our tastes, needs and aspirations.

They are socially active, however, they do not reveal themselves to the rest of us, nor do they get involved in groups' activities.

They dislike organized religions, politics, fanaticism, prejudices, stock markets, financial interests, publicity, vain public debates, egoism, and excessive authority.

It is not so easy to gain membership in their groups and societies. Membership is by invitation only.

Membership procedures and initiation process, formalities, and rituals are rigorous. Many applicants have failed because of the tests they had to go through.

47

2-Category Two:
The Mou-Na.rin "Mounawariin", "M'Noura-Iin".
Ana'kh/Ulemite.. It means the enlightened ones.
It is either a noun or an adjective.
From the Ana'kh word Mou-Na.rin, derived the Ulemite term Mounawariin, which literally means people of the light, or more precisely the illuminated ones.

The Mou-Na.rin are humans, and they live on earth.
They are a group of thinkers, philosophers and scientists. They are the custodians of important books and ancient manuscripts about the origin of mankind, the creation of the universe and human races, as well as a multitude of subjects pertaining to vital aspects of humanity, non-terrestrial-intelligent beings, Arwah, and other dimensions that are closely connected to humans, and non-humans.
The Mou-Na.rin can contact non-terrestrial beings and entities via several and multiple techniques and means.
They can read thoughts, foresee future events, and cure people from all sorts of illnesses and diseases. A group of philologists and linguists of alternative epistemology believe that the Ulemite term Mounawariin means the people who came from the fire, because the Ulemite term is composed of two words: Mouna or Min which means from, and Narin or Nar, which means fire.
Another group of scholars suggests that the term Mounawariin means people who are surrounded with light, especially around the top of their head, similar to the Buddhas, and saints, because the term is composed of two words:
1-M, pronounced Meh or Miin, which means from, or came from;
2-Noura (Niir in Ana'kh), which literally means light.
It can be found in several languages, including:
a-Proto-Hebrew/Hebrew with the word Menora, which means many things including light, candle, lamp, candelabra branches.
b-Proto-Aramaic/Aramaic/Assyrian with the words Nourah, Nour, which mean light, flash of light, brightness.
c-Arabic with the word Nour, which means light.
d-Ousmani, ancient Turkish with the word Nour, which means light.
e-Farsi/Persian with the word Nour, which means light, and specifically heavenly light.

f-Urdu with the word Nour, which means light, and quite often referring to a religious light and spiritual inspiration.

Thus the complete meaning of the term becomes: People of the light. In esoterism, occult, black arts, Freemasonry and ultimate knowledge studies, the word light means ultimate knowledge and enlightenment.

Bodhisattva in Sanskrit. In westernized version (Probably not totally accurate), they are called the Illuminati.

3-Category Three:
The Gayir-Mirayin "Gayrmirayim".

It is composed of two words:

- **a**-Gayir or Gayr, which mean without.
- **b**-Mirayin or Mirayim, which mean visible, and/or could be seen.

The general meaning (Verbatim) is: Those who you can't see.

The Gayir-Mirayin are the non-Physical Ulema.

They do not reveal themselves to us. They communicate with the physical Ulema on an exclusive basis through:

- **1**-Secret codes and a visual language.
- **2**-Ectoplasmic apparitions.
- **3**-Transmission of mind.
- **4**-Visitations through Ba'abs.
- **5**-Telepathy triggered by a "Conduit" implanted and activated in the brain' cells. Ordinary human beings are not trained nor prepared to communicate with them.

They can't see them, and they can't sense their presence, even though sometimes they are very close to them.

4-Category Four:
The Ari-Siin "Arishim".

It means the noble and strong guardians or attendants, also the giant spirits or minds of knowledge.

It is composed of two words:

- **a**-Ari, which means big; giant; powerful; attendant; guardian; superior; guide;
- **b**-Siin (Also Shi-yin), which means mind; spirit; ultimate level of knowledge and science.

49

From the Ana'kh Ari, derived:
- **a**-The Sumerian words A-ri, which means giants, Aris, which means a grant, and Arig, which means attendant;
- **b**-The Assyrian words Ari and Aria, which mean giants;
- **c**-The Hebrew word Ari, which means a lion, and the name Ariel, which means the lion of God (Ari=giant, and El=God);
- **d**-The Hittite word Ari, which means long.
- **e**-The Ulemite Ari, which means those who have.

The Ari-Siin live and evolve in various higher physical and non-physical dimensions.

And this includes the physically known universe, and the meta-cosmos (The world Beyond). They are neither human beings, nor spirits. They are pure wisdom and energy.

History synopsis: The Ulema group or brotherhood was created during the time of Hiram, the Phoenician King of Tyre and King Solomon's ally. The group included illustrious astronomers, astrologers, physicians, mathematicians, artists, scientists, metaphysicists, philosophers, authors, and lecturers from Sumer, Babylon, Assyria, Phoenicia, Syria, Palestine, Israel, Egypt, China, Turkey, Mongolia, and Greece.

Later on in history, leading figures of the Knights of St John of Malta, The Templars, The Wise Men of Arwad, and Hiram-Grand Orient Masonic Rites' members joined the Ulema group.

People are taught to believe that the world (Seen and unseen) consists of a physical life on Earth, and a spiritual life after death. The Ulema's views are different. According to The Book of Sun of the Great Knowledge, the world or universe usually referred to as "Wu-Jud" contains more than a physical life and a spiritual life. Wu Jud consists of 11 dimensions. Humans are aware of three dimensions only. Some have learned about additional dimensions through theoretical quantum physics, but their knowledge of these extra-dimensions is minimal, or simply theoretical.

The fourth dimension is the one that exists in the next life.

That is the limit of Man's understanding and interpretation of the world; the physical and non-physical (spiritual).

To the Ulema, life, the world, including human existence go beyond the fourth dimension.

For instance, the "Guardians" live in the fourth, fifth, and sixth dimensions. In the seventh and eight dimension, live the "Ultimate Ones", and so on...

Thus, the "Guardians" who live in higher dimensions are noble entities who communicate with chosen human beings and enlightened teachers for various reasons and purposes.

The "Guardians" are not physical beings, however, they can manifest to us in any shape or form using a "Plasmic" organism or substance that the human mind cannot comprehend. The Ulema receive knowledge and guidance from the "Guardians".

The Ulema group was also called the "Society of the Book of Ramadosh". The Ulema do not discuss religions.

Anzu: Sumerian/Akkadian. Noun. Also Panzu and Zu.
Name of the Sumerian guardian of Enlil's bathing room. Anzu was born in the mountain Hehe.

He was always depicted as a demonic figure with eagle's wide wings, and ferocious lion's pawns.

In the Sumerian language, Anzu was spelled Imdugud; it was later found that his name was pronounced Anzu, or Zu.

One day, while Ellil was bathing, Anzu stole the Tablet of Destiny and fled to the desert. The tablet had magical powers, and the person who owns it becomes capable of ruling the universe, and deciding upon the fate of people.

Ea persuaded the mother-goddess Belet-Ili to give birth to a divine hero to defeat Anzu.

Belet-Ili produced Ninurta and sent him into battle.

After a huge fight, Ninurta pierced Anzu's chest with an arrow, and recaptured the Tablet.

Finally, the Tablet of Destiny was seized by Marduk.

Anzu is usually depicted as evil, however, in the Sumerian epic of Lugalbanda, Anzu is kind, gentle and entertaining

The myth of Anzu: There are multiple versions about Pazuzu as Anzu, Zu, and Malak Taus, referred to as Malak Tawoos in the Arabic and ancient Turkish lore. In the ancient scriptures, he appears to be either half-demon/half bird, or as a form of demonic entity.

51

Anzu (Imdugug in Sumerian).

In the Sumero-Akkadian mythology, Zu is a divine demon-bird (half man and half bird), also referred to as Imdugud or Anzu.

He stole the "Tablet of Destiny" from the Anunnaki god Enlil, and hid it on the top of a mountain.

According to one passage in the Akkadian/Sumerian tablets, Marduk killed the bird, but in another passage, Ninurta killed him. Yet, in an old version of the Babylonian story, Ea/Enki, father of Marduk destroyed Zu.

Scene from the Epic of Gilgamesh showing Enkidu on the left with a spear, and on the right Gilgamesh killing the bird-man Anzu, with a dagger.

Anzu watering the "Tree of Life".

Ao: Ancient Assyrian. Noun. Name of a very ancient god of the air, the wind, and possibly the thunderstorm, found in several archaic Assyrian writings. Also known as Yaw in Ugaritic and Phoenician. The word Ao was written very differently on ancient slabs, and appeared under various names, such as Ilu, How, Haw, Yav, Yah, Yaw, and Yul. Tiglath Pileser said, "Yav ursanu rahiz kiprat aibi", which means, Yav you are the chief (Ruler), and the one who inundates the fields of the enemies. The words Il, Ilu, Eli and El, as found in Ugaritic, Phoenician, Aramaic and Hebrew writings mean god, master and lord. Yah, whether in its primordial ancient Assyrian or in Ugaritic form, is etymologically the prefix of the Hebrew word Yah-weh (Yahweh Elohim).

Apkallu: Akkadian/Sumerian. Noun.
In Akkadian mythology, the Apkallu were the seven (sometimes eight) sages who served kings as ministers. These sages were:
1-Adapa (U-an, called Oannes),
2-U-an duga,
3-E-me-duga,
4-En-me-galama,
5-En-me-bulaga,
6-An-Enlida,
7-Utu-abzu.

An Apkallu

55

Apollo. Apollo's missions and extraterrestrial objects.
An avalanche of claims rotating around various extraterrestrial spacecrafts and objects being spotted by American astronauts invaded the landscape of ufology; it encompasses UFOs, tunnels, domes, lights, circular objects, discs, and lunar structures.
And those sightings were either deleted from the astronauts-NASA official communications transcripts, and/or explained by NASA's scientists as anomalies, space debris, so on...
In fact, and as stated by Dr. Farouk El Baz, one of NASA's most noted scientists, "Not every discovery on the Moon and in outer-space was reported or announced."
And in many conversations exchanged between the astronauts and NASA, secret codes were used to refer to UFOs, unidentified crafts, strange lights, unusual flying objects of various shapes and dimensions, and extraterrestrial "structures" such as:

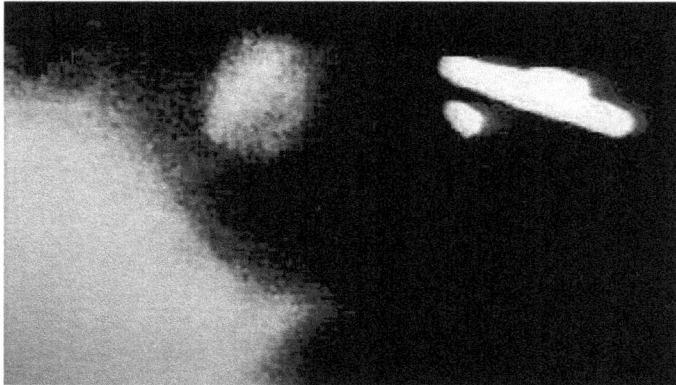

Photo of an unidentified cigar-shape flying object taken by astronaut John Glenn, Mercury 1 Mission, on February 26, 1962. Photo: NASA.

From the conversations exchanged between Apollo 16 astronauts and NASA on April 16-27- 1972:
Codes used:

1-Devices,
2-Blocks,
3-The blue one,
4-Beauty,
5-EMU,
6-PLSS,
7-Condor,
8-Alpha,
9-Condorset,
10-Condorcet Hotel,
11-Plum,
12-Barbara,
13-Kilo,
14-Bravo,
15-Babies,
16-Tango,
17-Jezebel,
18-Bogey. This code was also used by astronaut James Lovell during his flight on Gemini 7.

Below, is a brief excerpt from a conversation between Lovell and NASA:
Lovell: Bogey at 10 o'clock high.
Capcom: This is Houston. Say again 7.
Lovell: Said we have a bogey at 10 o'clock high.
Capcom: Gemini 7, is that the booster or is that an actual sighting?
Lovell: We have several actual sightings.
Capcom: Estimated distance or size?
Lovell: We also have the booster in sight...
17-Santa, so on.
In some instances, objects and structures on the Moon were mentioned verbatim by astronauts.

*** *** ***

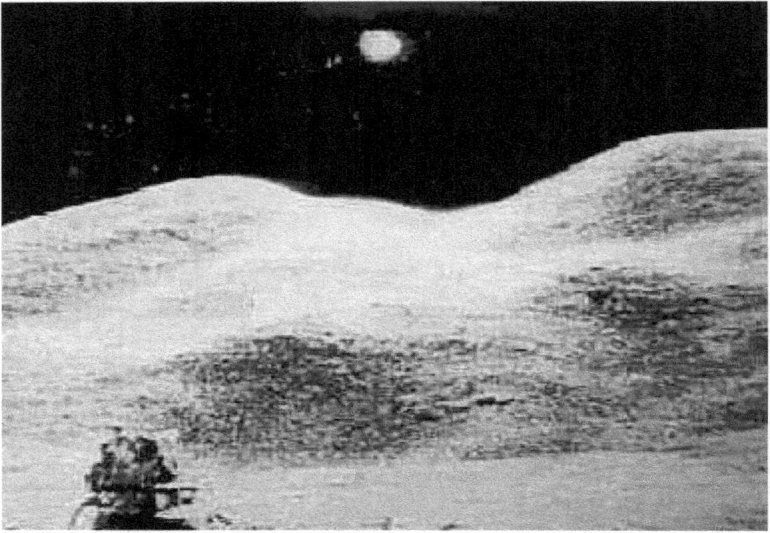

Neil Armstrong took this photo of a ball of light on the Moon. Photo: NASA.

Neil Armstrong took this photo in 1969. NASA explained this occurrence as "Space Anomaly"! Photo: NASA.

NASA's photo of astronaut David Scott on the slope of Hadley Delta, showing a bright circular object over the hills.

NASA's photo showing astronaut Charles Dukes walking on the surface of the Moon, and a UFO on the horizon.

A video footage taken during the second Apollo mission to land on the moon shows a disc approximately 100 miles above the surface of the moon. (Apollo 12, 1969. Photo: NASA.)

From the conversations of Apollo 11 astronauts:
Obtained via ham-radio independent operators bypassing NASA's secret broadcasting.
Astronaut Neil Armstrong: What was it? What the hell was it? That's all I want to know!"
Mission Control: What's there?... ... Mission Control calling Apollo 11...
Apollo 11: These babies were huge, sir! Enormous.
Oh, God! You wouldn't believe it! ...I'm telling you there are other space-craft out there... ...lined up on the far side of the crater edge! They're on the Moon watching us!
Astronaut Neil Armstrong: Those are giant things. No, no, no - this is not an optical illusion.
Astronaut Edwin Aldrin: No one is going to believe this!

Houston: What? What? What? What the hell is happening? What's wrong with you?

Astronaut Neil Armstrong: They're here under the surface.

Astronaut Edwin Aldrin: They're here.

Houston: What's there?

Note: Emission interrupted.

Astronaut Neil Armstrong: We saw some visitors.

Astronaut Edwin Aldrin: We saw some visitors. They were here for a while, observing the instruments.

Houston: Repeat your last information!

Astronaut Edwin Aldrin: I say that there were other spaceships.

Astronaut Neil Armstrong: They're lined up in the other side of the crater!

Houston: Repeat, repeat!

Astronaut Neil Armstrong: Let us sound this orbita ... in 625 to 5 ...automatic relay connected. My hands are shaking so badly I can't do anything. Film it?

Astronaut Edwin Aldrin: God, if these damned cameras have picked up anything what then?

Houston: Have you picked up anything?

Astronaut Edwin Aldrin: I didn't have any film at hand. Three shots of the saucers or whatever they were that were ruining the film...

Houston: Control, control here. Are you on your way? What is the uproar with the UFOs over?

Astronaut Neil Armstrong: They've landed here. There they are and they're watching us.

Houston: The mirrors, the mirrors...have you set them up?

Astronaut Edwin Aldrin: Yes, they're in the right place.

But whoever made those spaceships surely can come tomorrow and remove them. Over and out.

Note: Otto Binder, a former NASA employee stated that Buzz Aldrin said that he took a film footage of alien crafts, which was confiscated by the CIA. Neil Armstrong admitted that Aldrin did in deed took the footage of alien crafts, and he added that the CIA created a major cover of encounters with UFOs. This claim was confirmed in 1979 by Maurice Chatelain, then, chief of NASA Communications. Chatelain stated publicly that both Armstrong and Aldrin encountered UFOs on the Moon.

Maurice Chatelain said verbatim, "The encounter with UFOs was a common knowledge at NASA. All Apollo and Gemini Flights were followed by space vehicles of extraterrestrail origin or UFOs, if you prefer to call them that.
Every time an encounter occured, the astronauts informed Mission Control, and were ordered absolute silence..."

Maurice Chatelain
Maurice Chatelain believes that UFOs come from our solar system.

From the conversations of Apollo 15 astronauts:
Capcom: You talked about something mysterious...
Orion: O.K., Gordy, when we pitched around, I'd like to tell you about something we saw around the LM (LEM or Lunar Excursion Module). When we were coming about 30 or 40 feet out, there were a lot of objects - white things - flying by. It looked as if they were being propelled or ejected, but I'm not convinced of that.
Capcom: We copy that Charlie.

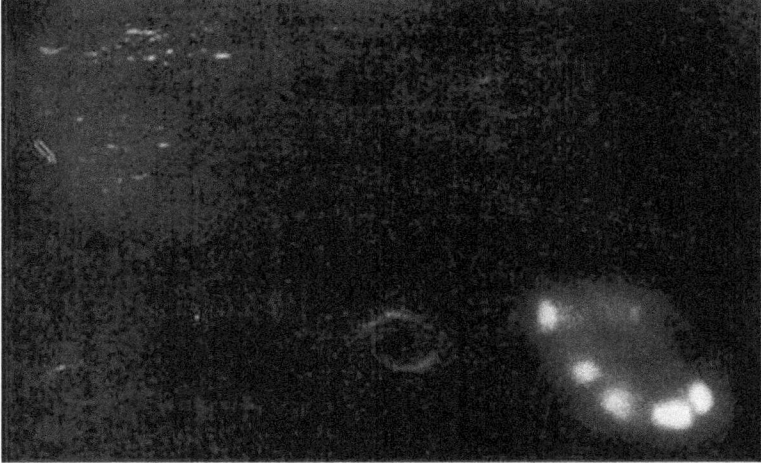

Photo of UFOs taken by Apollo 11 in 1971.

From the conversations exchanged between Apollo 16 astronauts and NASA on April 16-27- 1972:

Astronaut Charles Duke: We felt it under our feet...The scenery up on top of Stone Mountain, you'd have to be there to see this to believe it, those domes are incredible!

NASA Mission Control: O.K., could you take a look at that smokey area there and see what you can see on the face?

Astronaut Charles Duke: Beyond the domes, the structure goes almost into the ravine that I described and one goes to the top. In the northeast wall of the ravine you can't see the delineation. To the northeast there are tunnels, to the north they are dipping east to about 30 degrees.

Astronaut Charles Duke told NASA:

"Boy, I tell you, these EMUs and PLSSs are really super fantastic!" Right out here, the blue one that I described from the lunar module window is colored because it is glass coated, but underneath the glass it is crystalline, the same texture as the Genesis Rock. Dead on my mark...I can't believe it."

63

Photo taken by Apollo 15, showing astronaut James Irwin working on the Lunar Roving Vehicle, and an unidentified disc behind the hill in the background.

From the conversations exchanged between Apollo 16 astronauts and NASA:

Capcom: What about the albedo change in the subsurface soil? Of course you saw it first at Flagg and were probably more excited about it there. Was there any difference in it there - and Buster and Alsep and LM?

Astronaut Charles Duke: No. Around the Alsep it was just in spots. At Plum it seemed to be everywhere. My predominant impression was that the white albedo was (garble) than the fine cover on top.

Capcom: O.K. Just a question for you, John. When you got halfway, or even thought it was halfway, we understand you looped around south, is that right?

Astronaut John Young: That is affirm. We came upon.

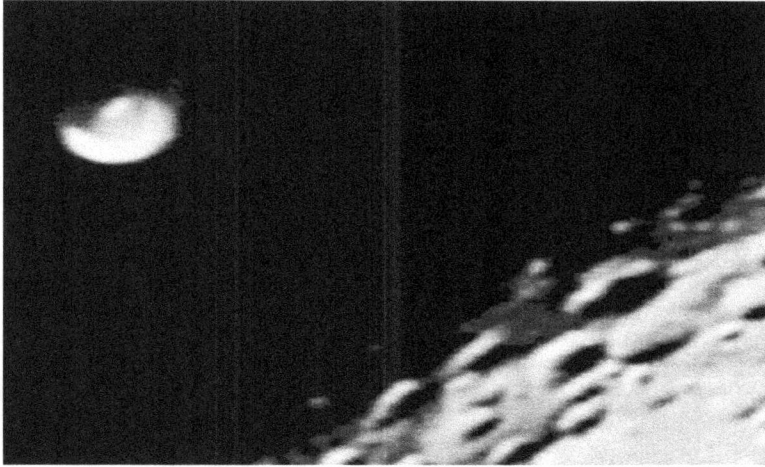

Photo of a UFO taken by Apollo 16. Photo: NASA.

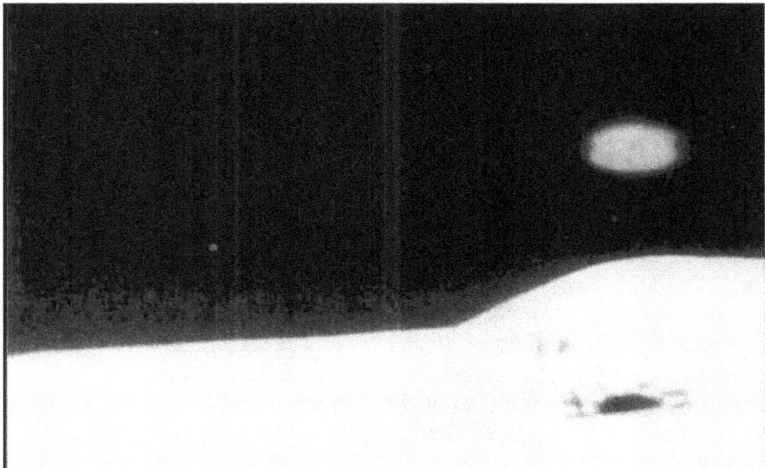

Photo of an unidentified flying object during the landing on the
moon, taken by Apollo 11. Photo: NASA.

From Apollo 16 astronauts and NASA:

Orion: I'm looking out here at Stone Mountain and it's got...it looks like somebody has been out there plowing across the side of it. The beaches - the benches - look like one sort of terrace after another, right up the side.

From the conversations exchanged between Apollo 17 astronauts and NASA on December 7-19, 1972:

Astronaut Ronald Evans told NASA: "I guess the big thing I want to report from the back side is that I took another look at the - the - cloverleaf in Aitken with the binocs. And that southern dome (garble) to the east."

Mission Control: We copy that, Ron. Is there any difference in the color of the dome and the Mare Aitken there?

Astronaut Ronal Evans: Yes there is... That Condor, Condorsey, or Condorecet or whatever you want to call it there. Condorecet Hotel is the one that has got the diamond shaped fill down in the uh - floor.

Mission Control: Robert. Understand. Condorcet Hotel.

Astronaut Ronald Evans: Condor. Condorset. Alpha. They've either caught a landslide on it or it's got a...and it doesn't look like.....in the other side of the wall in the northwest side.

Mission Control: O.K., we copy that Northwest wall of Condorcet A.

Astronaut Ronald Evans: The area is oval or elliptical in shape. Of course, the ellipse is toward the top.

From the conversations of Apollo 17 astronauts:

Lunar module pilot: What are you learning?

Capcom: Hot spots on the Moon, Jack?

Lunar module pilot: Where are your big anomalies? Can you summarize them quickly?

Capcom: Jack, we'll get that for you on the next pass.

Command module pilot: Hey, I can see a bright spot down there on the landing site where they might have blown off some of that halo stuff.

Capcom: Roger. Interesting. Very - go to Kilo, Kilo.

Command module pilot: Hey, it's gray now and the number one extends.

Command module pilot: Mode is going to HM. Recorder is off.

Okay, there's bravo. Bravo, select OMNI. Hey, you know you'll never believe it. I'm right over the edge of Orientale. I just looked down and saw the light flash again.
Capcom: Roger. Understand.
Command module pilot: Right at the end of the rille.
Capcom: You don't suppose it could be Vostok?

From the conversations of Apollo 17 astronauts:
LMP: OK. Al Buruni has got variations on its floor. Variations in the lights and its albedo. It almost looks like a pattern as if the water were flowing up on a beach. Not in great areas, but in small areas around the southern side, and the part that looks like the water-washing pattern is a much lighter albedo, although I cannot see any real source of it. The texture, however, looks the same.
Capcom: America, Houston. We'd like you to hold off switching to OMNI Charlie until we can cue you on that.
DMP: Wilco.
LMP: Was there any indication on the seismometers on the impact about the time I saw a bright flash on the surface?
Capcom: Stand by. We'll check on that, Jack.
LMP: A UFO perhaps, don't worry about it. I thought somebody was looking at it. It could have been one of the other flashes of light.Capcom: O.K., I copy on that, Jack. And as long as we're talking about Grimaldi we'd like to have you brief Ron exactly on the location of that flashing light you saw...We'll probably ask him to take a picture of it. Maybe during one of his solo periods.
DMP: O.K. 96:03. Now we're getting some clear - looks like pretty clear high watermarks on this...
CMP: There's high watermarks all over the place there.
LMP: On the north part of Tranquillitatis. That's Maraldi there, isn't it? Are you sure we're 13 miles up?
Capcom: You're 14 to be exact, Ron.
LMP: I tell you there's some mare, ride or scarps that are very, very sinuous, just passing one. They not only cross the low planar areas but go right up the side of a crater in one place and a hill in another. It looks very much like a constructional ridge...

From a conversation between astronauts and Houston Control in WAV format (241 Kb):

Astronaut 1: Ha! What is it?
Astronaut 2: We have some explanation for that?
Beeping sound.
Houston: We have not, don't worry, continue your program.
Beeping sound.
Astronaut 1: Oh boy it's a... it's, it, it is really something fantastic here, you, you could never imagine this!
Beeping sound.
Houston: Roger, we know about that, could you go the other way, go back the other way!
Beeping sound.
Astronaut 1: Well it's kind of...ha, pretty spectacular ... God ... what is that there?
Beeping sound.
Astronaut 1: It's...what the hell is that?
Beeping sound.
Houston: Go Tango, Tango!
Beeping sound.
Astronaut 1: Ha! There's kind of light there now!
Beeping sound.
Houston: Roger, we got it, we watched it, lose communication, Bravo Tango, Bravo Tango, select Jezebel, Jezebel.
Beeping sound.
Astronaut 1: ... Ya, ha! ... But this is unbelievable!
Beeping sound.
Houston: We call you up Bravo Tango, Bravo Tango!

Note:
Houston asked the astronauts to switch to a secret frequency, so no other outlets would be able to track the conversation between Houston and the astronauts.

*** *** ***

Statements by astronauts:
Major Gordon Cooper.

Major Gordon Cooper said: "For many years I have lived with a secret, in a secrecy imposed on all specialists in astronautics. I can now reveal that every day, in the USA, our radar instruments capture objects of form and composition unknown to us.

And there are thousands of witness reports and a quantity of documents to prove this, but nobody wants to make them public.

Why? Because authority is afraid that people may think of God knows what kind of horrible invaders. So the password still is: We have to avoid panic by all means."

Major Gordon Cooper

"I was furthermore a witness to an extraordinary phenomenon, here on this planet Earth. It happened a few months ago in Florida.

There I saw with my own eyes a defined area of ground being consumed by flames, with four indentions left by a flying object which had descended in the middle of a field. Beings had left the craft (there were other traces to prove this).

They seemed to have studied topography, they had collected soil samples and, eventually, they returned to where they had come from, disappearing at enormous speed...

I happen to know that authority did just about everything to keep this incident from the press and TV, in fear of a panicky reaction from the public."

Eugene Cernan

Eugene Cernan.

Eugene Cernan, commander of Apollo 17, said, "I've been asked about UFOs, and I've said publicly I thought they were somebody else, some other civilization."

Donald Slayton

Mercury astronaut, Donald Slayton stated: "I was testing a P-51 fighter in Minneapolis when I spotted this object. I was at about 10,000 feet on a nice, bright, sunny afternoon...as soon as I got behind the darn thing it didn't look like a balloon anymore.
It looked like a saucer, a disk...I tracked it for a little way, and then all of a sudden the damn thing just took off. It pulled about a 45 degree climbing turn and accelerated and just flat disappeared."

Neil Armstrong:
Armstrong stated, "The Aliens have a base on the Moon... and they told us in no uncertain terms to get off and stay off the Moon."

71

Neil Armstrong

Apsu: Sumerian/Akkadian/Mesopotamian. Noun.
Apsu and the beginning of the world.
Apsu is the watery deep beneath the earth. According to the Babylonian Epic of Creation (Enuma Elish, "When on High") at first, there existed only the male (Apsu) and female (Tiamat) gods of the deep. Apsu is a primeval Sumero-Akkadian god who personifies the primordial abyss of sweet waters underneath the earth. Apsu is the consort of Tiamat, the primordial abyss of salt waters of Chaos.

Yahweh link to the Apsu (The theme of water and the Hebrew Tehom): We learned from the Babylonian myths and poems that god Ea lives underneath Earth; a region that floats over the depot (Ocean) of fresh water, and which is found in the "Apzu", in the southern area of Babylon. According to the Mesopotamians, that region was the source and origin of all the waters on Earth.

And from that region emerged huge quantities of water in forms of streams.

This, made Ea (Enki) the lord (King) of waters, more precisely the "God of Waters" as described in the Mesopotamian clay tablets.

The word Enki is in fact an attribute, a title, an adjective, because is it composed of 2 words:

a-"En", which means King or God.

b-"Ki", which means Earth, as well as the underworld, and the land of no return.

God Ea sits over a throne of fresh waters.
In the Phoenician and Ugaritic myths, Bull-El or El resides deep inside a mountain, referred to by the ancient scribes as "Tehom", which is the source of the fresh and the salt water of the oceans, exactly as mentioned in the Anunnaki-Sumerian texts!
Thus, the Phoenician god is closely associated with water, rivers and the sea, similar to Enki who lives in the watery depths of the Apzu, which also is the source of freshwater rivers and streams.
In the Bible, Yahweh also sits on a throne of fresh waters.
The throne of Yahweh is placed on the top of stream of sweet and fresh waters, from the Temple in Jerusalem, all the way to the Dead Sea.
From the Sumero-Akkadian and Assyrian cuneiform clay tablets we know that Ea "Enki" created a huge fountain (A pond, a lake, a river) in the garden of Idin (Eden).

The Bible told us that Yahweh created a spring in the Garden of Eden (The same garden) which gave birth to four ancient rivers, called the Euphrates, the Hiddekel, the Pishon and the Gihon.
Numerous Mesopotamian slabs and seals depicted Ea "Enki" as an imposing god seated on an elevated throne with four or five streams of water (in the form of rivers) emanating from and/or around his shoulders. One of the characteristics and attributes of Ea is "God of water", frequently associated with "Apsu" which means in Sumero-Akkadian, ground-water.
Numerous Mesopotamian clay tablets depicted Ea "Enki" as a god inhabiting the "Apsu", and "Apsu" is where he dwells. As such, he is the universal creator, for water was needed to create the world.
In the Koran, we find a reference made to Allah as the creator of the universe, because he created water.
In the old-Babylonian epics, water played a paramount and primordial role; water gave birth to the world, and water through the Great Deluge destroyed the world. Unforgettable historical figures in the Sumero-Akkadian, Assyrian and Chaldean epics were commonly and frequently associated with water, such as Pirnapishtim (Also called Utnapishtim, Ziusudra and Atrahasis) who became the Hebrew Noah.

73

In fact, the Hebrew story of the Great Deluge is the same story of the old Babylonian Deluge, which is de facto, the flood of the Mesopotamian Euphrates River.

God Ea in the Apsu.

Aquarius Saucer: Name of an alleged secret project, which according to William Moore was created by the USAF to accumulate information, and data on alien life form, and UFOs.
Unfortunately, Aquarius Saucer Project was a fabrication by Mr. Moore, who managed to fool numerous ufologists.

Arabah: Hebrew. Noun.
A barren district, referring to the Jordan valley, extending from Mount Hermon to the Gulf of Akabah.
Religiously, Arabah is linked to Hathor the Lady of Byblos and the worship of the Golden Calf and Yahweh.

Painting of the worship of the calf by Nicolas Poussin.

_____

Stela of Lady of Byblos found in Byblos (Modern day Jbeil) in Lebanon.

The Egyptian Hathor which appeared seated on a large Egyptian throne was in fact the Phoenician "Lady of Byblos" (Modern day Jbeil in Lebanon) who was associated with the sun in Phoenicia, and who later gave birth to the imagery of the cow-sky-goddess in Egypt.

She was depicted as a golden calf and was worshipped at her shrines at Byblos, Har Timna in Arabah, and Serabit el Khadim in the southern part of the Sinai Desert. At one time in ancient history, she was a major goddess in the Egyptian pantheon.

The early Hebrews at one time worshiped their God Yahweh as a Golden Calf. It is obvious that the Jewish worship of the Golden Calf was inspired by Egyptian-Phoenician worship of Hathor-The Lady of Byblos and Canaanite rituals.

The Lady of Byblos as Hathor.

Arakh-nara "Arcturus": The name of a planet, unknown to legitimate science.

It is composed of two words:
- **a**-Arakh, which means portal or station;
- **b**-Nara, which means tar or light.

It was inhabited by the Anunnaki some 700,000 years ago. Many of us are not familiar with.

However, it was mentioned in channelers' séances and by Eastern ufologists, as well as by the Ulema.

Arakh-nara is known in the West as "Arcturus".

77

Edgar Cayce did mention it.

He stated: "...one of the most advanced civilizations in this galaxy. It exists in fifth-dimension and is the prototype for arth's future.

Its energies work as emotional, mental, and spiritual healers for humanity. The star is also an energy gateway through which humans pass during death and re-birth. It functions as a gateway station for non-physical consciousness to become accustomed to physicality.

Arcturus is a stargate through which souls pass, to choose whether to return to the Earth-sun system, or evolve to others."

Edgar Cayce

Arallu: Babylonian/Akkadian/Chaldean/Sumerian. Noun.
The land of the "Mountain of the World" where the gods and Enlil
were born. E-Kin "House of the land of the mountain" was the
oldest sanctuary in Northern Babylonia

Araya, time and the concept of: Araya is an Ana'kh word for
prediction; code. According to the Ulema, the Anunnaki's Araya is
an effective tool to foresee forthcoming events in the immediate
and long term future.
The expression or term "foreseeing" is never used in the Ana'kh
language and by extraterrestrials because they don't foresee and
predict. They just calculate and formulate. In spatial terms, they
don't even measure things and distances, because time and space
do not exist as two separate "presences" in their dimensions.
However, on Ashtari, Anunnaki are fully aware of all these
variations, and the human concept of time and space, and have the
capability of separating time and space, and/or combining them
into one single dimension, or one single frame of existence.

Anunnaki understand time differently from us, said the Ulema.
For instance, on Aldebaran, there are no clocks and no watches.
They are useless. Then you might ask: So, how do they measure
time? How do they know what time it is...now or 10 minutes later,
or in one hour from now? The answer is simple: If you don't need
time, you don't need to measure it. However, on Aldebaran, the
Anunnaki experience time and space as we do on earth. And they
do measure objects, substances, distances and locations as we do
on Earth. But they rarely do.

To calculate and formulate information and to acquire data,
Anunnaki consult the "Code Screen." Consulting the screen means
pragmatically, the reading of events sequences, explained the
Anunnaki Ulema.
Every single event in the cosmos in any dimension has a code; call
it for now Nimera, a "number", added the Ulema.
Nothing happens in the universe without a reason. The universe
has its own logic that the human mind cannot understand. In
many instances, the logic of numbers dictates and creates events.
And not all created events are understood by the extraterrestrials.

This is why they resort to the Araya Code Screen. Activating the Araya Code requires four actions or procedures:

1-Taharim: This demands clearing all the previous data stored in the "pockets" of the Net. A net resembles space net as usually used by quantum physics scientists. They do in fact compare space to a net. According to their theories, the net as the landscape of time and space bends under the weight of a ball rotating at a maximum speed.

The centrifugal effect produced by the ball alters the shape of the net, and consequently the fabric of space. And by altering space, time changes automatically.

As time changes, speed and distances change simultaneously. Same principle applies to stretching and cleaning up the net of the screen containing a multitude of codes of the Anunnaki.

2-Location of the Pockets: The word pockets means the exact dimension and a space an object occupies on the universe's net or landscape. No more than one object or one substance occupies one single pocket; this is by earth standard and human level of knowledge. In other parallel words, more than one object or one substance can be infused in one single pocket. But this could lead to loss of memory. Objects and substances have memory too, just like human beings; some are called:

a-Space memory,
b-Time memory,
c-String memory,
d-Astral memory,
e-Bio-organic memory, etc.

The list is endless. Thus, all pockets containing previous data are cleared.

3-Feeding the Pockets, also called Retrieving Data: All sorts and sizes of data are retrieved and stored through the Conduit.

The Conduit is an electroplasmic substance implanted into the cells of the brain.

4-Viewing the data: Retrieved data and information are viewed through the Miraya, also called Cosmic Mirror. Some refer to it as Akashic Records. Can the Anunnaki go forward in time and meet with the future? Yes, they can!

One Ulema said that future events have already happened at some level and in some spheres. It is just a matter of a waiting period for the mind to see it.

Arba: Ana'kh/Sumerian/Akkadian/Hebrew. Noun. Arba was one of the Nefilim leaders who built the city of Hebron, called Kiriath-Arba after him. (Josh 14:15; 15:13).
Arba was the father of Anak whose three sons, Sheshai, Ahiman and Talmai, were later arrested and expelled by Caleb, one of the commanders of Joshua.
The Hebrew scribes described them as follows: "These "Fallen Ones" were ferocious cannibalistic giants and had horrifying sexual relationships with women of the Earth, as well as with virgins, men, and beasts."

Arcana Arcanorum: Term for the three esoteric and hermetic freemasonary degrees, created by Cagliostro, and incorporated by Luigi d'Aquino into the Misraiim's rite in 1778. The masonic degrees were inspired by the three levels of the Anunnai Ulema, and the Brotherhood of Hiram, the Phoenician king who created freemasonary in Phoenicia.

Cagliostro

81

Archbishop Agobard of Lyons:
In a 9th century manuscript written in Latin, "Liber contra insulam vulgi opinionem", Agobard the Archbishop of the French city of Lyons, during the Carolingian Renaissance, discussed a popular belief in a region called Magonia, from which space-ships flew into the clouds, and were flown by pilots called "storms' wizards".

Apparently, French peasants believed that celestial crafts were flown by people who carried stolen vegetables and fruits from their harvest and were taken away to their land. Legend has it that three men and woman fell from the ships and were stoned to death by the peasants. Writers of the era believed that Magonia was the land of black magic inhabited by beings from another world.

Space-ships of Magonia.

Archetypes of UFOs and symbols, Carl Jung's: According to Carl Jung, father of the "Collective Unconscious" theory, UFOs could be linked to the symbol of mandala.

On July 30, 1958, the New York Herald Tribune, published a report by the Associated Press from Alamogordo, New Mexico, about Dr. Carl Jung's opinions of UFOs.

Here is an excerpt from the published article: Dr. Carl Jung, Swiss psychologist, says in a report released yesterday that unidentified

82

flying objects are real, and show signs of intelligent guidance by quasi-human pilots. "I can only say for certain that these things are not a mere rumour.

Something has been seen. A purely psychological explanation is ruled out". Dr. Jung, who had started his research on UFOs in 1944, issued his statement through the UFO-Filter Centre of the Aerial Phenomena Research Association (A.P.R.O.) here. He said: "I have gathered a mass of observations of unidentified flying objects since 1944. The disks do not behave in accordance with physical laws, but as though without weight.

If the extraterrestrial origin of these phenomena should be confirmed, this would prove the existence of an intelligent interplanetary relationship. What such a fact might mean for humanity cannot be predicted."

Dr. Carl Jung

Arcturus: See Arakh-nara.

Area 51: Also known as Groom Lake, and Dreamland, which is located approximately 90 miles north-northwest of Las Vegas in Nevada. It was originally chosen in 1955 by Lockheed's test pilot Tony LeVier to conduct testing for the spy-plane U2. The site was also used to develop and test the legenday Blackbird, SR 71, and the F117 Stealth Fighter.

Lockheed's test pilot Tony LeVier.

The legendary Blackbird.

Ufologists and conpiracy theorists claimed that Area 51 is where alien reverse engineering took place, and the U.S. government is conducting joint programs with the Grays-Aliens.

In 1952, President Dwight Eisenhower signed an executive order restricting the airspace above Area 51.

And for decades, the government denied its existence.

Additional nicknames for Area 51:

1-The Test Site.

2-Project 51.

3-Groom.

4-The Ranch.

5-Paradise Ranch, cined by Lockheed's Clarence Kelly Johnson, the designer of U2.

6-The Box.

7-Watertown Strip, coined by Richard M. Bissell, Jr., then head of the CIA's U2 Program.

Lockheed's Clarence Kelly Johnson, the designer of U2.

The first reference made to Area 51 appeared in a 1960 Lockheed's footage on Skunk Works preparation sheet for shipping A-12 prototype to Area 51, written by Kelly Johnson, and which contained the following note: "Move out to Area 51."

In 1995, President Bill Clinton signed an exempt order "PD" (Presidential Determination). The PD confirmed that Area 51 is exempt from all federal, state, interstate and local hazardous laws, which might require disclosure of secret and/or classified documents and information pertaining to Area 51.

See on the next page the "Presidential Determination" signed by President William J. Clinton:

THE WHITE HOUSE
WASHINGTON

September 29, 1995

Presidential Determination
No. _____ 95-45 _____

MEMORANDUM FOR THE ADMINISTRATOR OF THE ENVIRONMENTAL
PROTECTION AGENCY
THE SECRETARY OF THE AIR FORCE

SUBJECT: Presidential Determination on Classified
Information Concerning the Air Force's Operating
Location Near Groom Lake, Nevada

I find that it is in the paramount interest of the United States
to exempt the United States Air Force's operating location near
Groom Lake, Nevada (the subject of litigation in <u>Kasza v. Browner</u>
(D. Nev. CV-S-94-795-PMP) and <u>Frost v. Perry</u> (D. Nev. CV-S-94-
714-PMP)) from any applicable requirement for the disclosure to
unauthorized persons of classified information concerning that
operating location. Therefore, pursuant to 42 U.S.C. § 6961(a),
I hereby exempt the Air Force's operating location near Groom
Lake, Nevada from any Federal, State, interstate or local
provision respecting control and abatement of solid waste or
hazardous waste disposal that would require the disclosure of
classified information concerning that operating location to any
unauthorized person. This exemption shall be effective for the
full one-year statutory period.

Nothing herein is intended to: (a) imply that in the absence of
such a Presidential exemption, the Resource Conservation and
Recovery Act (RCRA) or any other provision of law permits or
requires disclosure of classified information to unauthorized
persons; or (b) limit the applicability or enforcement of any
requirement of law applicable to the Air Force's operating
location near Groom Lake, Nevada, except those provisions, if
any, that would require the disclosure of classified information.

The Secretary of the Air Force is authorized and directed to
publish this Determination in the <u>Federal Register</u>.

[Signed]
William J. Clinton

Area 51.

Are UFOs stored in tunnels under Area 51? Are these tunnels connected to secret aliens' bases?
There are no UFOs in underground tunnels. The tunnels are used for different purposes. There are approximately 25 underground tunnels below the main compound of Area 51. And they stretch all the way to Washington, DC, The White House, The Pentagon, the CIA, Langley, Virginia, NASA, Manhattan, Colorado, Maryland, Florida, Pennsylvania, Alaska, Hawaii, the Pacific, and Dulce. You name it.
They are everywhere!!
The UTTC (Underground Tram Transportation Central), also called Central Station, and the Tram is a 55 foot high by 45 foot wide compound of underground tunnels and trains connecting Area 51 to a web of secret undergrounds facilities and locations around the country.
Track TR1, like Air Force 1, is a direct track to The White House.
The red tunnel (TR2P) takes you directly to The Pentagon, and to Washington's National Airport. The 2 green tunnels take you to NORAD and Canada.
The gray tunnel (They call it actually "The Gray Line") takes you to Dulce Base. So there are no UFOs in the tunnels.

Area 54: Part of Area 51, which according to ufologists and conspiracy theorists is the precise location of secret spacecrafts tests and extraterrestrials' technology and reverse engineering.

Area S-4: Name of one of Area 51 facilities under the Papoose Mountains, according to Bob Lazar, and where United States' scientists worked on alien technology reverse engineering; reverse engineering of the technology of alien crafts.
Mr. Lazar has claimed that "the government possessed at least nine alien spacecraft at S-4."

Arecibo Message to extraterrestrials: On November 19, 1974, under the leadership of Dr. Frank Drake, founder of the 1960 Project Ozama, the Arecibo Observatory sent a message to the globular star cluster M13, which is 25,000 light-years away from Earth. The message consisted of 1679 binary digits, and was transmitted at a frequency of 2,380 MHz, with a power of 1,000

KWatt. The astronomers hoped that the message would/could be picked up by extraterrestrials and learn what Planet Earth is located. The message was written/designed by Dr. Frank Drake with the help of Dr. Carl Sagan.

It would take 25,000 years for the Arecibo's message to reach its destination, and an additional 25,000 years to receive any reply.

Earth's message to the extraterrestrials sent from Arecibo Observatory.

90

The Arecibo Observatory.

On its website, SETI posted the following, "Although it's unlikely that this short inquiry will ever prompt a reply, the experiment was useful in getting us to think a bit about the difficulties of communicating across space, time, and a presumably wide culture gap."

SETI on Dr. Frank Drake's attempt to communicate with extraterrestrials:

"In 1960, radioastronomer Frank D. Drake, then at the National Radio Astronomy Observatory (NRAO) in Green Bank, West Virginia, carried out humanity's first attempt to detect interstellar radio transmissions. Project Ozma was named after the queen of

91

L. Frank Baum's imaginary land of Oz -- a place "very far away, difficult to reach, and populated by strange and exotic beings." The stars chosen by Drake for the first SETI search were Tau Ceti in the Constellation Cetus (the Whale) and Epsilon Eridani in the Constellation Eridanus (the River), some eleven light years (66 trillion miles) away.

Both stars are about the same age as our sun. From April to July 1960, for six hours a day, Project Ozma's 85-foot NRAO radio telescope was tuned to the 21-centimeter emission (1420 MHz) coming from cold hydrogen gas in interstellar space. A single 100 Hz channel receiver scanned 400 kHz of bandwidth.

The astronomers scanned the tapes for a repeated series of uniformly patterned pulses that would indicate an intelligent message or a series of prime numbers such as 1, 2, 3, 5 or 7. With the exception of an early false alarm caused by a secret military experiment, the only sound that came from the loudspeaker was static and no meaningful bumps superimposed themselves on the formless wiggles on the recording paper.

After Project Ozma's pioneering steps, systematic searches for the technological manifestations of civilizations on the planets of other stars became a feasible scientific objective."-SETI.

SETI on the Arecibo's Message:

"In 1974, the most powerful broadcast ever deliberately beamed into space was made from Puerto Rico. The broadcast formed part of the ceremonies held to mark a major upgrade to the Arecibo Radio Telescope.

The transmission consisted of a simple, pictorial message, aimed at our putative cosmic companions in the globular star cluster M13. This cluster is roughly 21,000 light-years from us, near the edge of the Milky Way galaxy, and contains approximately a third of a million stars.The broadcast was particularly powerful because it used Arecibo's megawatt transmitter attached to its 305 meter antenna.

The latter concentrates the transmitter energy by beaming it into a very small patch of sky. The emission was equivalent to a 20 trillion watt omnidirectional broadcast, and would be detectable by a SETI experiment just about anywhere in the galaxy, assuming a receiving antenna similar in size to Arecibo's.

The message consists of 1679 bits, arranged into 73 lines of 23 characters per line (these are both prime numbers, and may help the aliens decode the message). The "ones" and "zeroes" were transmitted by frequency shifting at the rate of 10 bits per second. The total broadcast was less than three minutes. A graphic showing the message is reproduced here. It consists, among other things, of the Arecibo telescope, our solar system, DNA, a stick figure of a human, and some of the biochemicals of earthly life. Although it's unlikely that this short inquiry will ever prompt a reply, the experiment was useful in getting us to think a bit about the difficulties of communicating across space, time, and a presumably wide culture gap."-SETI.

Dr. Frank Drake writing his famous equation"
$$N = R^* \, f_p \, n_e \, f_l \, f_i \, f_c \, L$$

SETI's Explanation of Dr. Drake's Equation:

- **N** = The number of communicative civilizations
- **R*** = The rate of formation of suitable stars (stars such as our Sun)
- **f_p** = The fraction of those stars with planets. (Current evidence indicates that planetary systems may be common for stars like the Sun.)
- **n_e** = The number of Earth-like worlds per planetary system
- **f_l** = The fraction of those Earth-like planets where life actually develops
- **f_i** = The fraction of life sites where intelligence develops
- **f_c** = The fraction of communicative planets (those on which electromagnetic communications technology develops)
- **L** = The "lifetime" of communicating civilizations

Dr. Carl Sagan

Argus Project: On its website, SETI posted the following: "Project Argus, The SETI League's key technical initiative, has been called the most ambitious microwave SETI project ever undertaken without Government equipment or funding.

When fully operational, it will provide, for the first time ever, continuous monitoring of the entire sky, in all directions in real time.

What is Project Argus?

The name Argus derives from a 100-eyed being in Greek mythology. The search phase of *Project Argus* began on Earth Day, April 21, 1996, with just five operational radio telescopes. By November, 2000, the scope of our Argus equalled that of its namesake, with our 100th station actively participating.

Traditional research grade radio telescopes (the type which NASA used) can view only a small fraction of the sky at a given time, typically on the order of one part in a million. All-sky coverage with these instruments would thus require a million telescopes, properly aimed.

At a cost of perhaps one hundred million US dollars apiece, such a network would exceed the Gross Planetary Product.

Fortunately, there is another way.

Project Argus employs much smaller, quite inexpensive amateur radio telescopes, built and operated by SETI League members at their individual expense. A typical Project Argus station can be built for from a few hundred to a few thousand dollars, depending upon the expertise of the builder. Only five thousand of these smaller instruments, properly coordinated, are necessary to see in all directions at once.

The equipment, although of modest sensitivity, is still believed capable of detecting microwave radiation from technologically advanced civilizations out to a distance of several hundred light years."-SETI.

Ari: Sumerian. Noun. A royal title meaning the shining ones.

Ariani: Ariani entered the colorful literature of ufology and the paranormal when it was allegedly used for the first time by the legendary explorer Rear Admiral Richard B. Byrd in "Admiral Richard B. Byrd's Secret Diary." (February-March 1947).

Basically and essentially, the word Ariani is a term for the "inner world of the Earth." Some refers to it as the "Hollow Earth. Others call it the subterranean word of a highly advanced civilization unknown to us.

95

Rear Admiral Richard Byrd.

Originally, the alleged diary of Rear Admiral Byrd was produced in 1970s by an organization located in Missouri, USA, which called itself "The Society for a Complete Earth" headed by a Native American named Tawani Wakawa Shoush. Members of Rear Admiral Byrd stated publicly that the so-called Diary of Admiral Byrd is a fake, and "his lost diaries never existed."

Admiral Byrd's secret diary of his expedition to the North Pole in 1947 was discredited by Byrd's family members, historians, and archeologists.

Arizona lights, the: On March 13, 1997, a huge unidentified spaceship invaded the skies of Arizona, and was spotted by thousands of people, including the governor of the state.
The sighting was nicknamed the "Phoenix Lights".

The Arizona Lights. Photo by Dr. Lynne Kitei, who wrote a magnificient book, and produced a video footage on the "Phoenix Lights".

The "Phoenix Lights" are not anomalies, or otherworldly but rather the German "V6" as called by the USAF; it is the enormous German V shaped mothership-spacecraft "Die Mutterschiff Einsatzkommando" which is manufactured by the GNWO, in a no-fly zone in Canada. The same notorious no-fly zone controlled by German scientists who challenged President Harry Truman by a tour de force display of glowing circular-shaped objects which hovered over Washington, D.C. in 1952.

97

And the D.C. UFOs were totally unrelated to extraterrestrial UFOs, or to another world.

Civilians, ufologists and the general public will never know the truth about the "V6: Die Mutterschiff Einsatzkommando."

For revealing the truth will *sine dubio* create an immense and irreparable embarrassment to the United States, our military, our intelligence agencies, the United Kingdom, and expose the macabre "Triangle Commission", which serves as the executive committee of the New World Order!!

The "Phoenix Lights".

The "V6" is not something new. Dr. Edward Teller, father of the American H Bomb, and Dr. Openheimer, father of the American A Bomb submitted a preliminary report on the "V6" to President Harry Truman who assessed their report with close advisors and friends who were members of the "National Defense Research Committee", which consisted of Roger Adams, Vannevar Bush, K. T. Compton, James Bryant Conant, Alphonse Raymond, Albert Baird, Jerome Clarke, Frank B. Jewett, Alfred Newton, and Lewis Hill. Truman's National Defense Research Committee played a major role in UFOs' cover-ups.

Nota Bene: Worth mentioning that my sources suggested that some military scientists who were assigned to NASA, confound it "V6: Die Mutterschiff Einsatzkommando" with "Die Schwerkraft Aufhebemaschine", another anti-gravity spacecraft designed by German scientists after World War Two.

Arnold Kenneth's UFOs sighting:

On June 24, 1947, Kenneth Arnold took off from Chehalis airport. At 3:00 P.M., he spotted 9 silvery flying objects over Mount Rainier. Estimated speed of the flying machines: 1300 miles an hour.

What did he see?

Ufologists claim that Arnold saw extraterrestrial UFOs. They are mistaken! In fact, what he saw was a formation of 9 German Horten 229.

OBJECTS SEEN BY KENNETH ARNOLD

traveling this way

Top

NOTATIONS BY ARNOLD

FROM HIS LETTER TO THE

AIR FORCE, JULY, 1947

They seemed longer than wide, their thickness was about 1/20th of their width

traveling this way

Mirror Bright

(NOTE: he later reported that one object had a double crescent shaped rear end.)

They did not appear to me to whirl or spin but seemed in fixed position, traveling as I have made drawing. /s/

Kenneth Arnold's notations from his letter to the United States Air Force, July 1947.

Kenneth Arnold displaying an artist's illustration of one of the nine flying objects he saw in Washington State. In reality, the crescent-shaped UFOs he saw were German UFOs Horten 229. See pertaining photos on the next page.

_____

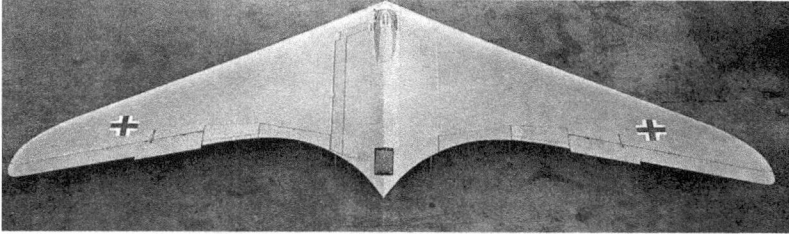

The German UFO Horten 229.

Kenneth Arnold's crescent-wing (Left) and the German original prototype Horten 229 (Right).

101

Horten types I, II, III.

A formation of 9 Horten 229 which flew over Washington State on June 24, 1947 was spotted and reported by Kenneth Arnold, who reportedly said "flying like a saucer would."

Kenneth Arnold in front of his airplane.

A German UFO Horten 229 (aka Hitler's stealth fighter) replica, re-designed and manufactured in late 2008, by engineers from Northrop Grumman.

Front of the anti-radar German Horten 229, as reconstructed
in the United States by Northop Grumman.

Engineers at Northrop Grumman. studied the remains of the only
surviving German wonder-plane, Horten 229, re-designed it,
rebuilt it, and tested its astonishing avant-garde stealth
capabilities, and later on, displayed it in public for a short time.

German Horten Wing UFO.

Northrop Grumman Corporation, the San Diego Air and Space Museum, and the National Geographic Channel teamed up to build a full scale of the German Horten 229 Flying Wing (Germany-World War UFO)

The original German *Horten 229 Flying Wing*.

The original German Horten 229 Flying Wing, at a United States government secret storehouse outside Washington, D.C. It was kept secret by the United States government for more than 50 years.

The German spacecraft was captured during the war's final days, by the American army in a top secret facility near Frankfurt, in Germany.

107

Young Walter Horten with his first Horten wing-plane in 1929.

The original Horten 229 flying wing invented by the Horten
brothers, unloaded by the United States army in 1945.

Walter Horten and Reimar Horten with their Horten Type I.

Artificial gravity and UFOs: Artificial gravity is a simulation of gravity in outer-space. According to NASA, Ames Perceptual and Behavioral Adaptation Group's, Malcolm Cohen, "Artificial gravity is a potentially useful tool, but it's not a universal panacea." According to ufologists, numerous abductees have reported the total absence of gravity inside an alien craft. And some have claimed that "there being an artificial gravity inside aliens' UFOs." Ufologists believe that the "UFOs' propulsion system generates centralized curvilinear gravitional field gradients."

Aruru "Mammi": Babylonian/Sumerian. Noun.
Aruru means Creative force; the creator of life.
From Aruru derived the Arabic word Rouh, and the Aramaic-Hebrew words Rouach, Rouah, Rohka, meaning soul. Aruru was the Babylonian great mother goddess of creation. Like so many other Sumerian gods, Aruru created Enkidu from clay in the image of Anu. With the help of Enlil, she created the first man. Aruru is also called the womb goddess.
Following the advice and instruction of Ea, she mixed the blood of the god Geshtu-e, with clay she found on the Euphrates river bank, and created seven women and seven men. She had to create the first "set" of primitive humans to do the physical work of the Igigi.

Arwad "Aradus": Phoenician/Ugaritic/ Greek.
An ancient Phoenician island in the Mediterranean Sea.
The Island of Arwad was an independent kingdom in the days of the Canaanites. It was created by the Phoenicians in early second millennium B.C. This small beautiful island located 5 miles from the city of Tartus in Syria, was one of the first Anunnaki's small colonies on earth.
It was mentioned in the Bible by the Prophet Ezekiel. Arwad was the headquarters of the seven wise men who came from Apsu, the sweet water, and attended the gods of Enki. They were known to the Sumerians as Abgal, to the Akkadians as Akkallu, and to the Phoenicians as An-Khal. The Anunnaki called them "The Ab-n'GAL."
On the Island of Arwad, the Phoenician created a secret society called the "Circle of the Serpent" to honor their god Melkart.
On Arward, the Melkart shrine/altar still stands in all its beauty and majestic architecture.

111

The early learned Greeks who visited Arwad studied medicine at the Phoenician-Anunnaki medical center, and when they returned home, they adopted the Phoenician sign of the serpent as the logo for their healing arts.

Arwad hold many secrets, to name a few:
1-For a short time, Jesus and Mary Magdalene lived there after the Biblical Crucifixion.
2-St. Paul sailed to Arwad after he has spent some time in Byblos (Jbeil) and Batroon in Phoenicia (Today, Lebanon).
3-It was at Arwad, that the Anunnaki created the "Brotherhood of the Serpent".
4-The Phoenicians had a secret society called "The Fish" and it was headquartered in Arwad.
5-The Templar Order used the island as a hide-out. In fact, Arwad sheltered the last Crusaders and the remnants of the Templar knights who fled France following their massacre on the hand of the king of France and the infamous Inquisition.
Some claimed that the Templar knights returned to Arwad to retrieve the Holy Grail; the genealogical tree of Jesus and a buried gospel by Mary Magdalene. Ironically, at one time in history, Arwad was Pope Clement V's gift to the Templar knights.
The Island of Arwad was the last stronghold of the Crusaders in the Near East.
6-During the French occupation of Syria and Lebanon during the Second World War, the Vichy French Government discovered Anunnaki-Phoenicians tablets buried underground in Arwad. The ancient tablets told the story of a race of super humans who descended on earth and taught the fishermen how to navigate the sea and how to read the maps of the stars.
They created a secret society called "Brotherhood of the Fish".
Later on in history, the "fish" became the secret symbol of early Christians. It was St. Paul who first created the fish symbol as a secret way for early Christians to recognize other Christians in the Levant, Greece and Rome.
In ancient times, Arwad was a refuge to many persecuted Phoenicians, Hebrews, as well as Greeks and Romans. It is a perfect spot for a modern time Ernest Hemingway. You will be intrigued by the layout of the island's houses and its fortress.

The Castle of Arwad.

The Castle of Arwad was built by the Knights Templar; it was one of the last refuges-shelters of the Crusaders. Some have claimed that the Templars returned to the Castle to retrieve the Holy Grail. Others have said, that esoteric Ulema Ijtimah (Reunions, meetings) took place at the castle under the guidance of the Mounawariin (Enlightened Ones, Honorable Masters), where metals transmutation into gold and precious stones occurred on a regular basis.

113

Phoenician tombs on the Island of Arwad (Syria).

Island of Arwad, where Phoenicians created a secret society called the "Circle of the Serpent" to honor god Melkart. Arwad is mentioned in the Bible by the Prophet Ezekiel.

A view of a Syriac Deir (Monastery) at Arward.

Arzawa: Hittite. Noun. Name of the ancient Hittite Kingdom in Cappadocia (Turkey), and the land of the early Hittites, who communicated with the Anunnaki, and other extraterrestrials.

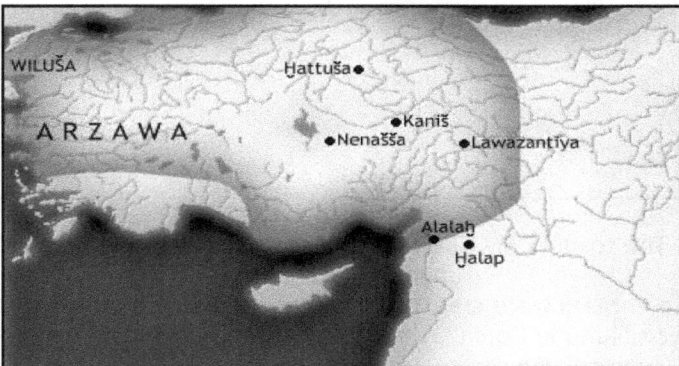

Map of Arzawa.

115

The town of Myra, one of the earliest Djinn and Afrit
strongholds in Anatolia.
These entities were created by the Anunnaki. According to the
book "Ilmu Al Donia", the Afrit constantly disturb Turkish
women who are known to be psychis and mediums.

Cappadocia, today.

AS2: A division of the British Ministry of Defence (MOD) which continued the operations of reporting on UFOs, previously carried on by the DS8.

Asherah: Ana'kh/Phoenician. Noun.
Name of a Phoenician-Anunnaki goddess, and the consort of the supreme god.
Asherah was known as "She Who Walks in the Sea," and was also called Holiness, and, occasionally, Elath, the goddess.

Asherah was an Amud (Pillar or column in Hebrew, Aramaic, Phoenician, and Arabic) with seven branches on each side surmounted by a globular flower with three projecting rays, and no phallic stone, as the Jews made of it, but a metaphysical symbol.

Ashera Amud (Pole) being destroyed by an Israelite.

According to the texts from Ugarit (Modern Ras Shamra, Syria), Asherah's consort was El, and by him she was the mother of 70 gods. As mother goddess she was widely worshiped throughout Syria and Palestine, although she was frequently paired with Baal, who often took the place of El in worship. As Baal's consort, Asherah was usually called Baalat.

118

Asherah, the 70 gods and the Anunnaki:
According to texts from Ugarit (Modern Ras Shamra, Syria), Asherah's consort was El, and by him she was the mother of 70 gods. As mother goddess she was widely worshiped throughout Syria and Palestine, although she was frequently paired with Baal, who often took the place of El in worship. As Baal's consort, Asherah was usually called Baalat.

The 70 gods, children of Asherah and El were astonishingly called "Binnin Ashira", after their mother, and not their father, the almighty god El. And there is a reason for this.

Asherah as a Phoenician goddess.

119

Ashera as a Jewish goddess.

Ashera as an Anunnaki-Phoenician goddess.

In the Anunnaki extraterrestrial society, the mother plays a paramount role. In fact, the Anunnaki society is a matriarchal society. And this very unusual and characteristic aspect, ties Asherah to the Anunnaki of Phoenicia.

Asherah was hated by the Jews for several reasons, but the two most important ones were:

1-Her Anunnaki extraterrestrial origin made her the offspring of the Biblical "Giants" (Anakim, Anunnaki), the enemy of the Tribes of Israel.

2-God El, her husband, who is a physical representation of an Anunnaki leader on Earth, was a direct threat to Yahweh, and consequently, a direct menace to their religion.

Ashlag, Yehuda Leib Ha-Levi (1885-1954): Hebrew. *Noun.*
A modern day Kabbalist and secret Anunnaki Ulema, Rabbi Ashlag was born in Warsaw to a family of scholars that had been part of the great Hassidic courts for generations.

As a child of seven, Ashlag secretly studied the Kabbalah – a forbidden subject, since the study of the subject was limited to scholarly married men over forty. He apparently managed to do so by hiding pages from the book *Etz Chaim (Tree of Life)* by the great Kabbalist Isaac Luria, between the pages of the Talmud, which he was supposed to be studying. Not that he neglected his Talmudic and biblical study – by the age of nineteen he was given the title of rabbi by the other rabbis of Warsaw, a rare honor. He even worked as a judge in the rabbinic court.

It is interesting that Ashlag was also interested in secular studies – enough to make him learn German and study the works of several philosophers. Between the ages of nineteen and thirty-six there is much mystery regarding his life. He was studying with a teacher that was never named, and was assumed to be a Kabbalist – but it is entirely possible that this was the Anunnaki-Ulema teacher that trained him to be one himself.

In 1921, he decided to move to the Land of Israel. For three years he supported his family doing physical labor, studying and writing his commentaries at night, but in 1924 his work became famous and he became a rabbi. Ashlag continued with his Kabbalistic studies, eventually writing (mostly while staying in London) a book of commentaries on his childhood's favorite book – Isaac Luria's *Etz Chaim.*

121

He continued to interpret the master's other works, but actually developing his own startling views on the subject.

The book is over two thousand pages, divided into sixteen parts, and it is considered to be the core of teaching Kabbalah.

In addition to this work, he had a group of students that gathered to learn and practice Kabbalah, and even created a Kabbalistic newsletter.

His efforts were different from all other Kabbalists before him in that he did not wish the Kabbalah to be a hidden, secret subject. Rather, he wanted to reveal and explain and make it a way of life. He had an idea that this was the only way to save man from his own tendency for evil and encourage his spiritual values.

In addition to his religious work, Ashlag had strong political views. He was anti-capitalist and anti-imperialist, and had a leaning toward Marxism, but staunchly objected to forced communism, such as in the Soviet Union. He had a vision of a religious version of libertarian communism, based on Kabbalistic principles.

The community he wanted was based on love and economic justice, and therefore was a supporter of the kibbutz movement and even international communes. He fiercely objected to any form of brute force regime.

He was not interested in material possessions for himself, and his loving kindness toward everyone was legendary. It is interesting to note that like so many other Jewish great mystics, Ashlag died on Yom Kippur. —From the Book "Anunnaki and Ulema Who's Who", co-authored by Maximillien de Lafayette and Dr. Anbel.

Ashtari Constellation: Anunnaki's habitat (Planet, stars, etc.) See Aldebaran.

Ashur: Assyrian/Sumerian/Babylonian/Akkadian. Noun.
Also called: "Ashir", "Assur", "A-sir", "Arusar", "A-shar", "Asu", "Aššur", "A-šur", "Aš-šùr", "Asshur", "Ashar", "Asar".
Name of the supreme god of Assyria and god of war.
Ashur was the king of the Igigi. His symbol is a winged circle or a globe with the human figure of a warrior god, armed with a bow in its center.
Ashur in the Bible:
Genesis 10:10-12: "And the beginning of his kingdom was Babel, and Erech, and Akkad, and Calneh, in the land of Shinar.

Ashur as the King of Babylon dressed into an Anunnaki motif.

Out of that land went forth Asshur, and built Nineveh, and the city Rehoboth, and Calah, And Resen between Nineveh and Calah: The same is a great city."
Isaiah 30:31:"For through the voice of the Lord Assyria will be beaten down, As He strikes with the rod."

123

The tombs of the Middle Assyrian kings at Ashur.

Zephaniah 2:13: "And He will stretch out His hand against the north, Destroy Assyria, and make Nineveh a desolation, As dry as the wilderness."

Zechariah 10:11: "He shall pass through the sea with affliction, And strike the waves of the sea: All the depths of the River shall dry up. Then the pride of Assyria shall be brought down, and the scepter of Egypt shall depart."

Ezekiel 32:22: "Asshur is there and all his company: His graves are about him: all of them slain, fallen by the sword."

Cylinder seal with the Anunnaki solar disk of Ashur, with two eagle-headed gods before the Tree of Life.

The Anunnaki wing of Asshur appeared in many ancient inscriptions and on statues of various civilizations and centers of worships, from Guatemala to Ghotic cathedrals in France, and from pillars in Persian and Roman palaces to Phoenician altars and fortresses of Crusaders in Malta, Cyprus, Syria, Turkey, Jordan, and Lebanon.

The Symbol of Ashur depicting the three manifestations of Elohim or God. Ashurai kings were servants of God. They were the first king-priests of ancient times.

Ashur's temple called E-Kharsg-Kurkurra in Ashur was one of the wonders of Assyrian architecture.

Ashur: Assyrian/Sumerian/Babylonian/Akkadian/Aramaic. Noun. Name of the ancient city of Kala Sherghat, which was the most ancient capital of the Assyrian kingdom. Around, 1,300 B.C., Shalmanesser I, deserted it to build Calah as the new capital of Assyria.

In 1100 B.C., Tiglath-Pileser I, brought Ashur back to its former glory, and declared it the new capital of Assyria.

A tunnel leading to a mound at Shergat.

An entrance to the fortress of Shergat.

Ashurbanipal "**Assur-Bani-Pal**": Assyrian. Noun.
Name of an Assyrian king (668-626 B.C.), and son of Esarhaddon.
He is known in Greek writings as Sardanapalus and as Asnappeer
or Osnapper in the Bible.
Ashur-Bani-Pal is famed for his magnificent library at Nineveh,
which contains literary treasures and magnificent epics/poems
about the Anunnaki-Sumerian-Assyrian gods and goddesses.

129

A slab depicting musicians and attendants of Ashurbanipal.

Relief of King Assur-Bani-Pal (Ashurbanipal) reposing with his queen in the Royal Garden, gypsum, North Palace, Nineveh. From the Neo-Assyrian Period, 1000 B.C.- 612 B.C.

Assur-Bani-Pal's extensive library contains a collection of 20,000 to 30,000 cuneiform tablets, and approximately 1,200 distinct texts. It was not the first library of its kind, but it was one of the largest and fortunately one of the most important libraries to survive to the present day. Most of it is now in the possession of the British Museum or the Iraq Department of Antiquities.

*** *** ***

Stone panel from the Palace of Ashurnasirpal II, Nimrud, circa 883-859 B.C.

Stone panel from the Palace of Ashurnasirpal II, 883-859 B.C.

Assur-Bani-Pal building his city.

A photograph of Tablet 4 of the Epic of Gilgamesh. From the
Library of Ashurbanipal, king of Assyria 669-627 B.C.

Tablet of the Sumerian Flood Story. 19th-18th century B.C.
From Assur-Bani-Pal library.

Tablets of the Creation.

The Seven Tablets of Creation contained an in-depth depiction of Apsu, found among the literary treasures of Assur-Bani-Pal.

Asket: Name of a female alien transplanted on the landscape of ufology by Eduard "Billy" Meier, who according to Meier belongs to an extraterrestrial race called the Timars, and who guided him for 12 years, and taught him the secrets of the universe.

Meier produced a photograph of Asket and published it in his 1983 book "UFO...Contact from the Pleiades Volume II."; a striking tall woman with sparkling blond hair, and elongated earlobes.

Unfortunately, and as expected, it was later discovered that the photograph of alien Asket belonged to singer and dancer Michelle DellaFave, who appeared on The Dean Martin Show (1969-1973).

Meier's blurry picture of the female alien Asket. Photo's caption by Meier et al, "This is a photograph of Asket, a cosmonaut from the Dal Universe who first had contact with Meier in India in 1964 and helped him prepare for the Pleiadian contacts that would occur eleven years later."

"Here is the truth about these photos. The person identified on the left as Asket is actually the singer and dancer Michelle DellaFave. Michelle was a longtime member of the "Golddiggers" and the "Dingaling Sisters" who appeared on the Dean Martin Variety Show from 1969-1973.- "Independent Investigations Group". The IIG is an international network of trained investigators who will not only look into paranormal, fringe science, and extraordinary claims in their own regions, but also administer the IIG $100,000 Challenge.

From IIG's website: "Michelle wrote to me and said that "Nera" was actually Susan Lund.
Susan appeared on the Dean Martin Variety Show from 1968-1973. This is what Michelle has to say on the situation:
"I know that the picture of myself and Susie is from the Dean Martin show when the Golddiggers were guests on the show. I think it is about 1971 and I did wear my hair with little curls at the side of my face. It amazes me that he chose that picture. I guess it was when they did the reruns in Europe. I do not want anyone thinking I am causing any problems.

138

Astarte "Ashtaroot", "Ashtaroth" (Sumerian Ishtar):

Phoenician/Semite/Babylonian/Akkadian/Hebrew.

Name of the principal goddess of the Phoenicians, representing the productive power of nature.

Astarte was a moon goddess and was adopted by the Egyptians as a daughter of Ra or Ptah.

In Jewish mythology and Judaica, she is referred to as Ashtoreth, and sometimes considered the wife of Yahweh.

Astarte

Astarte

Astarte was known and worshipped under so many names and titles by the Phoenicians, Akkadians, Babylonians, Sumerians, and Greeks.

Astarte was the most important female deity in a multitude of pantheons. The Persian form of the word is Astara. Ashtaroth and Ashtaroot in Phoenician.

The Sumerians and Akkadians called her Ishtar. Another form of the name afterward appeared in Greek mythology as Asteria.

Ashtaroth was also called Ashtoreth, Ashtaroot, Astarte, Ishtar, Ashtarte in multiple pantheons of the ancient world.

Ashtaroth was the Phoenician moon goddess worshipped in many civilizations, starting with the ancient Canaanites.

In the Pheonician pantheon, Ashtarte or Ashtaroot was the main goddess of the Sidonians. The Phoenician colonies carried the worship of Ashtoreth into the Mediterranean.

Her different names:
1-In the Old Testament, she is called Ashtoreth (Amorite-Hebrew noun). Linguistically and traditionally it is a name given by the Hebrew scribes to the old Semitic mother-goddess.

The Hebrew word Ashtoreth is derived from Ashtart by a distortion after the analogy of "Bosheth".
2-In Phoenicia, she was called Ashtaroot and Ashtarte;
3-In Babylonia, Ishtar;
4-In Arabia, Athtar;
5-In North Africa, she was known as Tanith (Barton, "Semitic Origins," p. 253), to which is frequently attached the epithet "Face of Baal," showing that she was often regarded as sub-ordinate to that god.
6-In Carthage, she was also Dido (Love), and was, as Augustine says ("De Civitate Dei," ii. 4), worshiped with obscene rites (Heb. x. 48-53).
7-In Babylonia and Assyria she was worshiped as Ishtar at several different shrines. Erech was one of the oldest and most important of these shrines, where she was called also Nanâ, and generally appears as the goddess of sexual love and of fertility.
8-At Agade, she was worshiped as the wife of Shamash ("Heb." x. 24-26), and at Babylon the wife of Marduk

*** *** ***

Stela of Ashtaroth.

Astra: Code for the triangular shaped tactical reconnaissance TR-3B aircraft, which became operational in the early 90s. The plane was funded by the National Reconnaisance Office, the NSA, and the CIA. At the early stage of its flight, authors of books on UFOs, and numerous ufology's enthusiasts believed that the TR-3B was an extraterrestrial UFO.

TR-3B aircraft.

143

TR-3B

Astraglossa: A term for a language (Lincos) for extraterrestrial communications, also called Lingua Cosmica, developed by Hans Freudenthal, a distinguished professor of mathematics at the University of Utrecht.

Astraglossa is based in part upon an extension of mathematics' logistic language initiated by Bertrand Russell, and Alfred North Whitehead.

Grosso modo, Astraglossa is a mathematical language which could in theory, be used to communicate with aliens, more precisely extraterrestrial intelligence.

144

Professor Hans Freudenthal.

Alfred North Whitehead

Bertrand Russell

145

Astral plane, and the astral aliens' equation: "Astral aliens" is an esoteric concept which is shared by a great number of channelers, psychics and ufology's enthusiasts, and proposed the avant garde theory of the esoteric, spiritual, and occultic aspects of aliens' nature. Thus, according to lightworkers, a spiritual and psychic contact with aliens is possible.

Some have even claimed that healing could occur via channeling with aliens. In its January 2014 Issue, Extraterrestrials Magazine (Published by Times Square Press, and Maximillien de Lafayette), included an interview with leading lightworkers and psychics in the United States, including Patti Negri, the First Lady of the Occult, and Senior Vice President of the American Federation of certified Psychics and Mediums, on the spiritual and esoteric aspect of this subjet.

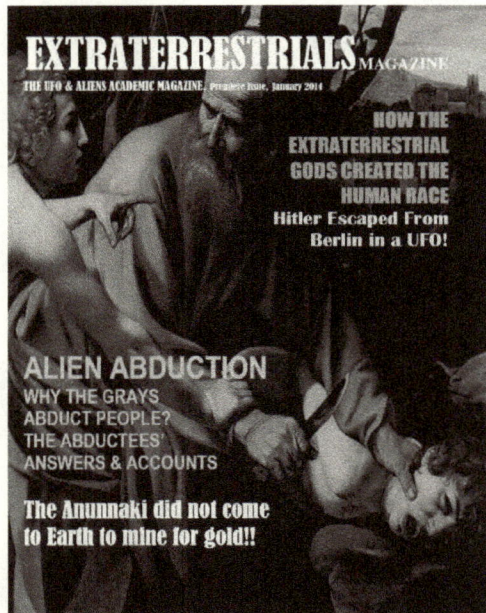

Cover of Extraterrestrials Magazine which published interviews with some of the world's most distinguished lightworkers, mediums, and psychics, such as Van Doren Figueredo, Patti Negri, Sunhee Park, and Chinhee Park.

146

Herewith excerpts from said interviews.

Interview with Patti Negri:
Q: You said "Aliens are all the talk amongst lightworkers right now." In what respect? And why lightworkers should be interested in aliens?
Patti Negri: Yes, it is a newish phenomenon to me of the past few years. We have certainly been aware of the alien realm for a long time, but it seems like it is actually coming into our psychic awareness, work and visions a lot more now. I believe that it is due to the thinning of the veil that is going on now and everything is just becoming clearer. Religious, spiritual and scientific worlds are colliding into one in so many ways – that these are exciting times indeed. As the veil lifts and we see the other realms clearer and clearer it makes perfect sense that the alien world would surface as well. I do think it is important that many lightworkers are interested in aliens. Just as angels seem to be making a bigger "comeback" with lightworkers these last several years.
They are both a part of our past, present and future – and in so many ways are the thing that is tying together so many cosmologies and belief systems. I realize that aliens are not every light workers 'cup of tea" – and that's okay. There are many roads to heaven – but I think we are now at a time where they are going to openly make themselves known – and the humans need to be ready or at least aware!

Q: Being the matriarch of the occult world, have you ever heard about "Lightworkers' Aliens Channeling?
Some lightworkers are claiming that Aliens can provide some sort of therapy via channeling. What is your take on this?
Negri: Yes, I have heard of it, in fact I have personally experienced it on a couple of occasions. It is indeed very different than other being or entity channeling. Heavier, denser, choppier and just plain different. I am an energy worker/shifter. I work with energy fields and flows.
Alien energy is quite a bit different than that of a deceased human spirit or other entity. Séances are one of my specialties – I have been doing them since I was 7 or 8 years old. This past year I did my first Anunnaki séance. I called in specific Anunnaki entities by name.

147

The great Patti Negri, voted best medium in the world (2013-2014), and best psychics in the United States (2013-2014).
Photo credit: Arturo Castillo.

We did sounds, sentences, sayings, sigils and chants I learned from Maximillien de Lafayette's books! Wow! The energy, the spirits, the sounds – everything was so much different than any other session I have ever had. There were about a half a dozen of us there. Each person had a different and profound experience of the evening. It was eye opening, magical and enlightening.

I do believe there is therapeutic value in alien channeling. But, like any other life force, being or entity – you have to be discerning of who you are talking to. Aliens, like other spirits or entities can be bad or good. Wise or simple.

Truthful or tricksters...so, the same way you are careful at who you invite into your home, we must be careful of the "wisdom" or messages we are getting. It is so funny to me, we people are so careful of who or what we absorb or listen to as wisdom. But as soon as it is "otherworldly" of any kind – we automatically think they have some sage wisdom or truth. In my experience, there is some real false or misleading "tricksters" out there – in every realm of existence, so just use your own intuition and sense to know who or what to listen to – and take as "truth".

Q: Is it possible for some lightworkers to channel via Aliens? Well, they do it via Angels as they often claim? Anything outside the perimeter of terrestrial boundaries is alien. What do you think? Some have claimed that aliens, spirits and angels share the astral and spiritual realm? What is your opinion on the subject?

Patti Negri: Yes, as stated above, I have personally channeled alien energy on a few occasions. As with any entity, I think it can be helpful or not! As far as aliens and angels, I see everything as energy.

I put less importance on words or titles. In my years of study, I believe that the belief systems or cosmologies we each choose to go by are what we use as a road map to chart the universe, our spiritual lives and the unknown.

They are markers or guide systems for us to wrap our still developing human brains around so we can understand the bigger picture a bit better. Yes, angels and aliens are on a different astral, vibrational and spiritual realm than we are.

Though, I believe many humans are hybrids of angels and/or aliens.

Whether we call it ancestral blood line, witch blood, alien or angel bloodlines. I think there is truth in all of it.
If we go deep below the words, again – what I get is energy.

From the interview with Sunhee Park:

From left to right: Sunhee Park, movie star Nia Peeple, and Chinhee Park.

Sunhee Park: Aliens are the talk because there are certain levels of understanding the spiritual world. The more awake we become, the more we can see and hear.
Aliens are the last and final step to really getting the big picture, and since we are in tune with the other dimensions, why would we not be in tune with the dimensions that aliens exist in?

We are intrigued by them, we want to know more about their existence, their intelligence, and why they are here. There is more evidence from ancient history to the present that has proven that they exist, and lightworkers do not base anything on the tangible. We are the ones who tap into the unknown and exercise it daily. We are the prime candidates to be able to communicate with them as we can with the crossed over, alive spirits, read minds, and astral travel and so on.

150

Lightworkers are interested in aliens because they are the highest of source to provide pertinent information on how to save this earth, planet, and human life.

They are advanced and unconditional, (well the good ones). They are in the highest of dimensions to help humans to become evolved and all around. I have actually experienced in real life that alien channeling is healing for the client. I don't think that every psychic can channel alien transcripts or even understand what is going on, it is different then spiritual channeling. The body gets very heavy and you are in a trance like state as if an alien is morphing into your body and mind. Then the other difficult thing is that they do not speak clear English, and they show us visuals and make noises that a very good psychic who is able to relay the messages as clear as possible in the English language. You cannot just make up stuff that you think you hear, and there has to be a common respect and clear way of asking questions to them.

I worked with a client for a total of 60 hours on chat channeling alien messages to a client. This happened over a period of months, and the messages were not clear, but the little ones that I did get, she got something out of it and also started to look at her problems in the present. She was living in the other dimensions and did not like human life that it took probably 7 psychics to help her and heal her from this alien channeling technique that she wanted.

She did not want a psychic reading, only alien channeling. She was also part E.T. and definitely had an E.T. soul. If I did not see the healing occur, I would say ET channeling is bogus. But I saw it live in person, and I feel that not everyone can do it. Alien Channeling is brand new to us, but practice makes perfect.

Who is to say it will not be a niche down the road? I do predict the future, so I do see it becoming more and more needed for alien abductees, or people who take UFO's and alien topics in a negative way. The more knowledge out there, the less scared people will be. The trick too is to make sure you identify which alien race you are calling upon, because like mediumship and calling in spirits, you can attract the negative ones as well. I definitely saw them coming in trying to manipulate the messages in my chats with the client. It was an obvious change of degrees, and my body felt so heavy that it was a dark entity trying to stop me from giving my client messages.

151

I was also in a very heavy trance-like state and I know I was in another dimension. I also do not remember what I was typing, and my computer would have glitches, pauses, multiple words typed out that I did not type, and it knocked my website off of the server. This is not evidence of poltergeist, this was when I was channeling and receiving ET information.

Aliens are angels to me, and human spirits have a different feeling to them. They are full of more emotions, dysfunction of physical ailments and ego.

Aliens do not feel sick, or have ailments, are not overly sensitive and their voices are like robots or machine like, they are not like a human voicebox and they do not speak English.

They also are telepathic, so that is why I was able to relay messages because I have practiced telepathy and ESP for 15 years. Angels have a different feel to them, but they are not like human spirits. There are differences to distinguish, but if you channel aliens and keep practicing to apply it to your readings, healings, and energy work, good stuff will come out of it. The aliens are coming closer to reveal themselves, and there will always be a war with the good and the bad. The good aliens want us, the lightworkers to relay information so whether you believe your alien guide is an angel or human spirit and its working well for you, then that is what level of understanding you are on. But if you feel that aliens are in another dimension and you feel them around, then accept that you are going up and up in understanding the bigger picture. There is so much to understand than what the eyes can see, and once you do get to alien channeling, you will see that its Deeper than the Pacific Ocean.

There are mountains that have life in them, underwater, and beyond the 3rd dimension. It is awesome and to keep learning and channeling is what I intend to do. ESPsychics has 6 psychics that are willing to do alien channeling, and I encourage those who want to do it to learn, it only makes you a better and well rounded person.

From the interview with Chinhee Park:
Chinhee Park Yes, aliens are the talk amongst lightworkers. It seems to be a topic that we are all very interested in. Lightworkers should be interested in aliens as they are a higher power to us and help guide us like spirits do.

They have influenced us and our abilities and I believe could be responsible as to why we are truly gifted. We may not have tangible evidence or proof, but to me it feels right and makes sense that the aliens are protecting and guiding us.

I have heard of many Lightworkers channeling aliens.

It's becoming more and more known. A lot of lightworkers do not publicize it for fear of what society will say or be judged. I agree with the lightworkers who claim that Aliens can provide some sort of therapy via channeling. They know when we are tuning into them, channeling them or talking to them telepathically. They are healers and will heal you emotionally and physically.

I strongly believe they are a part of us as we are a part of them.

I strongly believe it is possible for some lightworkers to channel via aliens.

Those that can channel via aliens come from alien DNA. I have an alien guide and he has shown himself to me. Not crystal clearly, but enough for me to know he is there to help me. I believe Aliens, Angels and spirits share the astral and spiritual realms. We are all connected somehow and we can tap into the dimensions and realms that angels, spirits and aliens are in. I believe evolving to the highest level is when you believe in aliens and seeing the big picture. Not needing to have tangible evidence but keeping an open mind that we, human beings are not the only species that exist and our dimension is not the only one that exists. A lot of us lightworkers and people in general have witnessed, experienced and connected with other species and dimensions.

When you are open, accepting and loving anything is possible.

Psychic Van Doren Figueredo's statement:
Van Doren said, "Aliens are definitely reaching out to many lightworkers today in order to assist with the activation of Alien Therapy, which takes shape and metamorphoses in numerous and various forms of dreams, teleportation, and implants.

I have heard of lightworker's Alien Channeling and I know it has been in existence for centuries.

Based upon my own recent personal experience, this form of Channeling is very therapeutic and informative, for it helped me reconnect in a deeper level to myself, and allowed me to tap into ancient eras and past history, and especially the missing link to time's passages in recorded history of humanity."

153

Van Doren Figueredo

Van Doren Figueredo added, "I encourage lightworkers who have an open mind explore this ability. Lightworkers are the "natural" choice and "expected candidates" for Alien Channeling.
It is possible for lightworkers to channel via aliens and to pass on, a rich avalanche of extra-dimensional information with absolute clarity.
This type of channeling is similar to a certain degree to Angels' Channeling. Consequently, Alien Channeling could be helpful to many, and allow lightworkers in the healing souls' process.
My channeling via aliens increased my own psychics and spiritual abilities; it is not different from connecting with your Angels.

In my opinion, lightworkers are chosen to do the task, and are selected to serve as a conduit. Simply put, Alien Channeling is one of the many forms of channeling with beings from a higher dimension or even from a parallel world."

154

Astro-biolectric robots: Also called B.E.R. (An acronym for Bioelectric extraterrestrial robots.)
The topic of bioelectric robots (or astro-biolectric robots) isn't often addressed by astrobiologists, however astro-geneticists in general have shown some interest in exploring this new field of study. Only ufologists are psychologically prepared to go one step further. See B.E.R.

Astrobiology: The study of extraterrestrial life.

Astronauts and cosmonauts' sightings of UFOs:
See Apollo. Apollo's missions and extraterrestrial objects.

Astronomical explanations: See UFOs' sightings.

Astronomical Observatory and Marseille's UFO plasma engine: Three leading French physicists have publicly claimed that they have made an extraordinary breakthrough in the mysteries of how UFOs are powered.

Dr. Jean-Pierre Petit

The scientists stated that Dr. Jean-Pierre Petit, Dr. Maurice Viton, and Dr. Claude Poher have built a UFO's engine, called "The Petit-Viton Magnetohyrodynamic Motor", by using nuclear power and electromagnetism.

Dr. Claude Poher

Apparently, the UFO plasma engine was built at the Astronomical Obervatory in Marseille, France.

Dr. Jean-Pierre said, "It all comes down to standard physics. An electromagnetic field can create a low pressure area under an aerodyne, or flying saucer.

To this can be related the peculiar property of plasma. Plasma's magnetic field is frozen inside while it expands at unimaginable speeds, producing an electrical current.

Using plasma, a belt of 'free air' can be created. The molecules of air in front of this belt are pushed aside without piling on top of each other, as they do when a normal aerofoil passes through the atmosphere fast enough to break the sound barrier.

We're not saying we've solved the problem, but we think we have cracked the principle behind the effects observed in unidentified-flying- objects". More on the subject can be found in the papers of Groupe d'Etudes des Phenomenes Aerospatiaux.

Astronomical Unit: The scientific measurement of space. One astronomical unit is referred to as the distance of 149,597, 870.691 kilometers from Planet Earth to the Sun.

Astrophotographic video footage of US-extraterrestrial officers: Some ufologists, conspiracy theorists, and so-called Pentagon's insiders-whistleblowers have claimed that some of the stars are in fact extraterrestrial stations, and spaceships piloted and manned by "Extraterrestrial Officers".

Some have suggested that there are hundreds of extraterrestrial satellites orbiting Earth.

These assumptions were widely and solely based upon an alleged "Astrophotographic video footage of US-extraterrestrial officers" shot by John Lenard Walson, which according to conspiracy theorists and some ufologists has revealed a new and mysterious "categories" of satellites totally unknown to scientists, and which are piloted by alien astronauts.

Ufology's legend has it that the United States government was very disturbed by Walson'discovery, and unmarked black helicopters were constantly hovering over his home.

Jeff Rense wrote, "This is - possibly - a profoundly important development. If Mr. McKinnon's data and assumption are correct, it validates what I and others have been postulating for many years: that the US Navy/Military may well be operating off-planet via back-engineered ET technology (or WWII German?) for a long time...long enough to have a 'fleet' of space craft and officers to either man them or otherwise control them.

Pics from Walson's footage, allegedly still frames of spaceships
(Space-flying machines).

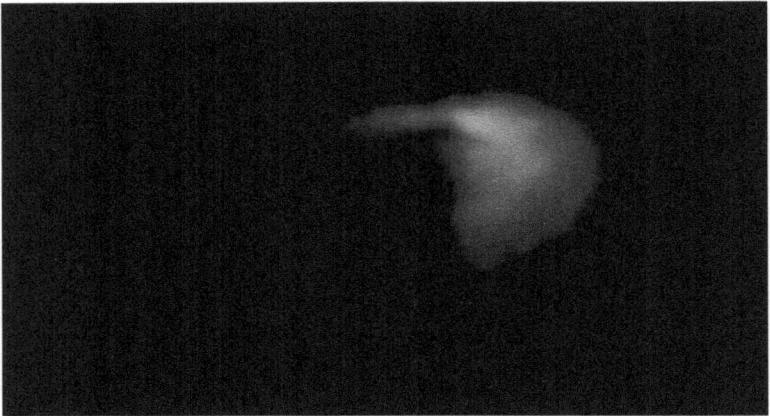

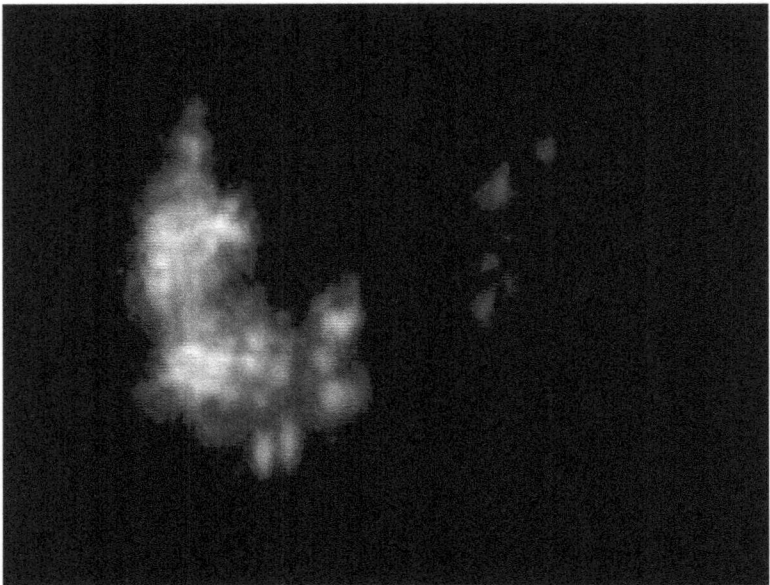

Pics from Walson's footage, allegedly still frames of spaceships
(Space-flying machines).

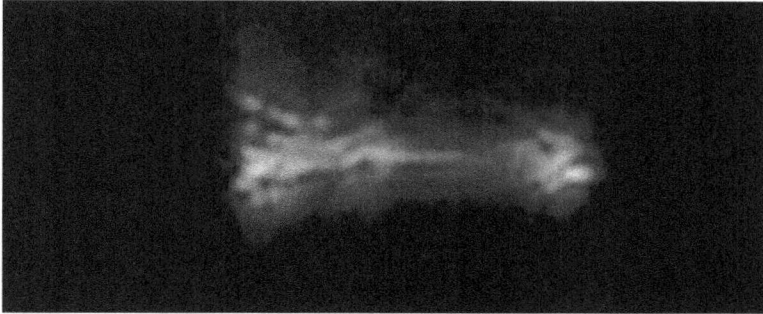

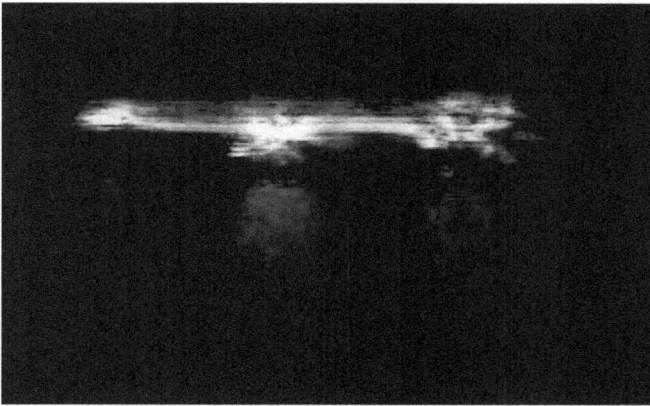

For those who remember the Clementine mission, you will recall
it was a US Navy project which micro-mapped the entire Moon.
If McKinnon stumbled onto a secret file of 'Non-Terrestrial
Officers'...it would, indeed, suggest the US Military has been
quietly, efficiently, secretly running off-planet operations for a
long time." Unfortunately, the discovery of Mr. Walson was later
found to be a hoax!
Yet, many ufologists still believe that the footage of Mr. Walson
was genuine, and his discovery is the real McCoy!

159

AT: Acronym for the Alliens' Transcripts.

The Aliens' Transcripts (AT) are a collection, a record, a detailed account, a huge dossier on all the meetings with non-human entities that occurred from 1947 to the present.

The Aliens' Transcripts have a paramount military significance and an enormous national security importance.

The Aliens' Transcripts (AT) contain thousands upon thousands of pages, sketches, illustrations, charts, graphs, communiqués, notes, statistics, secret Presidential orders, addenda, revised, and re-revised and updated addenda on everything pertaining to encounters and meetings with aliens.

However, the AT do not include civilians' encounters with aliens, abductions or UFOs' sightings.

AT are strictly and exclusively transcripts of meetings with aliens, extraterrestrials, and intraterrestrials.

From mid to the end of 1947, the Aliens Transcripts were a straight documentation and minutes of meetings with aliens in general; extraterrestrials, and intraterrestrials (The Grays).

In 1948, the Air Force and the Pentagon jointly decided to divide the Transcripts into three categories or parts, and as follows:

Category one/Part One: The meetings. This category recorded all questions and answers, and what it was decided upon to do or to continue to do during the meetings.

The minutes contained all the topics and subjects discussed, the material studied, and especially those of a military and scientific nature, names, ranks and titles of people (military and civilians) who were present, followed by recommendations and brief reports from scientists.

Issues, discussions and subjects on religion, ethics, Earth history, and anthropology were later incorporated in category three/part three. This decision was made by a two stars general following studies and reports submitted to his office by a committee of physicians, psychiatrists, and experts in behavioral sciences, who at the time, were working on esoteric, mind control, and psychosomatic projects and research.

Category two/Part Two: The projects:

This category refers to research programs, projects, and training sessions administered by two offices especially created by the military and The White House.

In this category, detailed reports on "Progress" were submitted by trusted military contractors, and added to the Transcripts.
On this, my lips are sealed.

Category three/Part Three: Addenda and reports. This category gathered and catalogued all sorts of information on aliens':
1-Nature.
2-Races.
3-Species.
4-Origin.
5-Habitat.
6-Technology.
7-Future operations.
8-Reports from military personnel at all levels on their personal rapports with aliens who worked with them in military bases.
9-Study and analysis of the behavior of the aliens.
10-Habits.
11-Strengths and weaknesses.
12-Nutrition.
13-Reactions in confined places.
14-Reactions/attitudes under severe weather conditions (Cold and heat).
15-Confrontations and debates with scientists, the military, and military guards.
16-Flights' tests.
17-Reverse engineering, so on.

Who had or has access to these transcripts?
Even 4 star generals could not access these transcripts. President ...tried and failed. Senator...did everything he could to have a glance at AT and he was "sent away".
Vice President...inquired about AT, and he was told, there is no such thing as Aliens' Transcripts. A congressional hearing was scheduled to inquire about AT and conduct some sort of questioning, deposition and investigation, but 2 two days later, it was cancelled.

At one time, Dr. Hynek tried to have access to the Transcripts and the Pentagon said: NO!

161

But Dr. Werhner von Braun, Dr. Edward Teller, Dr. Oberth, Albert Einstein, two young German scientists who are still around (They worked with Viktor Schauberger), and a young and brilliant scientist (Still alive) who worked with the late Karl Schapeller, had plenty of time and opportunities to go through the files of the Transcripts.

In 1948, we heard that Rudolph Schriever joined the scientists' team, although some colleagues have claimed that Schriever never participated in any project, simply because he died that year in Czechoslovakia. In 1951, Alberto Fenoglio, joined the team.

Twenty years later, Dr. Carl Sagan, and a very famous scientist (Still alive) known for his mind-bending theory on galactic civilizations were added to the roster.

ATD: Acronym for alien transportation device.

ATECH: Acronym for alien technology.

ATIC: Acronym for Air Technical Intelligence Center, located at Wright Patterson Air Force Base in Dayton, Ohio, which originally initiated Project Blue Book. In 1951, the Center was established to study Soviet technology.

In July 1961, the United States Air Force deactivated the center, to give birth to the National Air Intelligence Center (NAIC).

Officially, NAIC established on October 1993, and integrated the 480th Intelligence Group, and the Foreign Aerospace Science and Technology Center.

The Air Technical Intelligence Center played a paramount role in shaping the future of UFOs.

Atrahasis: Aka "Pir-napishtim", "Utnapishtim", "Ziusudra", "The Biblical Noah": Greek, Sumerian, Akkadian, Assyrian, Chaldean, Hebrew. Noun.
Nouh (Nuh) in Arabic.
Nuh in Turkish.
Nuh (Nuuh) in Farsi (Persian).
Nuh in Urdu.
Noach in Hebrew.
Noach in Tiberian.

From the Mesopotamian tablet: Line 8 to line 196:
"God Ea spoke to Utnapishtim who lived in Shuruppak,
And told him to build a ship to save himself
And his family from the coming flood."

In the Babylonian epics, god Ea warned Atrahasis about a flood that will decimate the world and annihilate the human race, and instructed him on how to build a boat to save himself and his family.
In the Bible, God Yahweh told Noah to build an ark of cypress wood and make rooms in it and coat it with pitch inside and out. Genesis 6:14,
"Build a large boat from cypress wood
And waterproof it with tar, inside and out.
Then construct decks and stalls throughout its interior."

Ea even gave Atrahasis precise instructions on how to build the boat, including height, length, width, etc. The Babylonian tablet provided us with a clear description of the interior of the boat.
The tablet specified that the boat should have six decks and seven levels, and include a divider;
"Dividing the whole interior of the boat
into nine compartments."

In the Bible, Yahweh told Noah the very same thing, and gave him the measurements of a boat he should build to save himself and his family. God told Noah how to make a boat, and gave him precise instructions.

The biblical vision of Noah and his boat.

Genesis 6:13,
"And God said to Noah, "I have determined to make an end
of all flesh, for the earth is filled
with violence because of them;
now I am going to destroy them along with the earth."
Genesis 6:14,
"Make yourself an ark of cypress wood;
make rooms in the ark, and cover it
inside and out with pitch."

The Christians' vision of the Deluge.

Genesis 6:15,
"This is how you are to make it:
the length of the ark three hundred cubits,
its width fifty cubits, and its height thirty cubits."

Genesis 6:16,
"Make a roof for the ark,
and finish it to a cubit above;
and put the door of the ark in its side;
make it with lower, second, and third decks."

Worth mentioning here that archaeologists discovered sediments and deposits of a flood in the Mesopotamian region which occurred in 2900 B.C., and concluded that the flood was indeed the flooding of the Euphrates river. According to historians and scholars, the Biblical flood occurred circa 2300 B.C.

There is a difference of approximately 600 years between the Babylonian flood and the Biblical flood. It is very clear that the Hebrew scribes borrowed the story of the Great Flood from the Mesopotamians.
The earliest story of the flood appeared in the "Epic of Atrahasis" and was recorded on three clay tablets during the reign of Babylonian king Ammi-saduga, 1647-1626 B.C.
A second story of the Babylonian flood appeared in the "Epic of Gilgamesh", circa 1100 B.C.

In Tablet XI of the "Epic of Gilgamesh", the Anunnaki god Ea spoke to Utnapishtim and said to him:

"Man of Shuruppak, son of Ubar-Tutu,
Tear down the house (Utnapishtim's house) and build a boat.
Leave behind possessions (Wealth) and seek the living people
Bring inside the boat,
the seeds of all living creatures.
The dimensions of the boat you shall build
must be equal to each other.
The length of the boat should equal the width of the boat."

Bringing animals to the boat:
God Ea instructed Utnapishtim to bring inside the boat, all the animals he could find around him, wild and not wild.

In Tablet XI, passage 35, god Ea said:
"Bring in the sheep inside the boat...
birds, cattle, and the creatures of the land..."

In the Babylonian Atrahasis, we read:
"On board of the boat (Inside the boat),
he brought all the creatures (Animals) of the field."

In the Bible, Genesis 6:19,
"And of every living thing, of all flesh,
you shall bring two of every kind into the ark,
to keep them alive with you;
they shall be male and female."

Genesis 6:20,
"Of the birds according to their kinds,
and of the animals according to their kinds,
of every creeping thing of the ground according to its kind,
two of every kind shall come in to you,
to keep them alive."

Genesis 8:16-17,
"Bring out every kind of living creature...
the birds, the animals, and all the creatures."

Chapter II, Genesis 7:2,
"Take with you seven pairs of all clean animals,
the male and its mate;
and a pair of the animals that are not clean,
the male and its mate..."

Chapter II, Genesis 7:3,
"And seven pairs of the birds of the air also,
male and female, to keep their kind alive
on the face of all the earth."

Chapter II, Genesis 7:8,
*"Of clean animals, and of animals
that are not clean, and of birds,
and of everything that creeps on the ground."*

Chapter II, Genesis 7:9,
*"Two and two, male and female,
went into the ark with Noah,
as God had commanded Noah."*

Chapter II, Genesis 7:14,
*"They and every wild animal of every kind,
and all domestic animals of every kind,
and every creeping thing that creeps on the earth,
and every bird of every kind,
every bird, every winged creature."*

Chapter 9, Genesis 9:10,
*"And with every living creature that is with you,
the birds, the domestic animals,
and every animal of the earth with you,
as many as came out of the ark."*

The dove:
Another striking similarity between the Babylonian story and the Hebrew story is the mentioning of the dove. In the Babylonian Tablet XI, we read that a dove was released from the boat to find a dry land, exactly as it is written in the Bible.

Here is an excerpt from the Babylonian text:
*"On the seventh day, I released a dove,
the dove flew but came back.
Then I released a swallow,
and the swallow returned.
Then I sent a raven but did not return."*

In the Epic of Gilgamesh, line 147, we read:
*"I (Utnapishtim) sent forth (out of the boat) a dove.
The dove went off, and came back to me."*

In the Bible, we read:
"He (Noah) sent forth the dove out of the ark,
and the dove came back to him."

In the Babylonian Epic of Gilgamesh, line 153, we read:
"I (Utnapishtim) sent forth a raven."

In the Bible, we learned that Noah sent forth a raven. The Bible told us that Noah released a dove from his boat, and the dove returned to him, and once again he sent off the dove, and when the dove returned to him carrying an olive branch, Noah knew that the dove found a dry land.

Chapter 8, Genesis 8:7,
"And sent out the raven;
and it went to and from until
the waters were dried up from the earth."

Chapter 8, Genesis 8:8,
"Then he sent out the dove from him,
to see if the waters had subsided
from the face of the ground."

Chapter 8, Genesis 8:9,
"But the dove found no place to set its foot,
and it returned to him to the ark,
for the waters were still on the face of the whole earth.
So he put out his hand and took it
and brought it into the ark with him."

Chapter 8, Genesis 8:10,
"He waited another seven days,
and again he sent out the dove from the ark."

Chapter 8, Genesis 8:11,
"And the dove came back to him in the evening,
and there in its beak was a freshly plucked olive leaf;
so Noah knew that the waters
had subsided from the earth."

Chapter 8, Genesis 8:12,
"Then he waited another seven days,
and sent out the dove;
and it did not return to him any more."

Summary:
The birds are set free:
The Mesopotamian tablet: Lines 145-155: Utnapishtim told us that the birds were set free to find out if the waters receded. In the Bible, Noah too sent a dove to find out if the waters receded.
The boat resting on the top of a mountain: A passage from the Bible referred to Noah's ark which rested on the top of Mount Ararat, as the flood began to go down.

Chapter 8, Genesis 8:4,
"And in the seventh month,
on the seventeenth day of the month,
the ark came to rest on the mountains of Ararat."

In the Babylonian epic, at the end of the flood, the boat of Utnapishtim lodged firm on Mount Nimush.
In the Babylonian Epic of Gilgamesh, we read:
"The boat lodged firm On Mount Nimush."

The Mesopotamian tablet: lines 131-143 describe how:
"The storm calmed down
and the ship rested firm on Mount Nisir."

Destroying mankind: In the Babylonian Genesis of Eridu, Tablet XI, line 98, we read:
"The gods decided that mankind
shall be destroyed."

In the Bible, Genesis 6:13, we read:
"And God said to Noah,
I have determined to make an end of all flesh,
for the earth is filled with violence because of them;
now I am going to destroy them along with the earth."

170

Chapter 6, Genesis 6:7,
"So the Lord said, I will blot out from the earth
the human beings I have created
people together with animals and
creeping things and birds of the air,
for I am sorry that I have made them."

Chapter 6, Genesis 6:17,
"For my part, I am going to bring
a flood of waters on the earth,
to destroy from under heaven all flesh
in which is the breath of life;
everything that is on the earth shall die."

Reason for sending the flood:
The Sumerian clay tablets told us that the Anunnaki sent the flood to annihilate mankind, because their noise (clamor) was disturbing their rest and sleep.

But the Assyro-Babylonian texts told us in Tablet XI of the Epic of Gilgamesh, that the gods sent the flood because the people of the city of Shurippak were wicked and corrupt.
Hereby are excerpts from a dialogue between Gilgamesh and Utnapishtim (The Hebrew Noah).

Utnapishtim talking to Gilgamesh:

"I will reveal to you, O Gilgamesh,
the mysterious story,
and the mystery of the Anunna (The Gods).
The city of Shurippak,
as you know is located
on the bank of the Euphrates River.
This city was wicked (corrupt),
so that the Anunna (The gods) living within it
decided to bring a deluge."
This Assyrian version coincides with the Biblical story of the deluge in Genesis.
Never again to bring a flood to earth and destroy mankind:

171

After the flood the Anunnaki gods decided to bring peace and safety to Earth, and the assembly of the Mesopotamian gods (The Anunnaki) promised to never again send a flood, and destroy the human race.

The Biblical story told us that after the flood, Yahweh blessed Noah and promised him to never again bring a flood and destroy mankind.

Genesis 9:15,
"I will remember my covenant that is between me
and you and every living creature of all flesh;
and the waters shall never again become
a flood to destroy all flesh."

Genesis 9:16,
"When the bow is in the clouds,
I will see it and remember the everlasting covenant
between God and every living creature of
all flesh that is on the earth."

Genesis 8:21,
"And when the Lord smelled the pleasing odor,
the Lord said in his heart, I will never again
curse the ground because of humankind,
for the inclination of the human heart
is evil from youth;
nor will I ever again destroy every
living creature as I have done."

However, there is a nuance's difference; the Anunnaki gods felt sorry for bringing the great flood, and many of them were in tears, because so many people were killed.

Per contra, Yahweh did not express any regret for bringing the great flood and annihilating humankind, because humans were wicked and deserved such a severe punishment.

The 7th day of the flood: In the Babylonian Atrahasis, we read:
"On the seventh day of the flood."

172

On a Babylonian slab, hundreds of years older than the Bible:
The Sumerian-Akkadian Noah (Utnapishtim, Ziusudra) in his
boat.

In the Bible, Genesis 7:10,
"after seven days the waters of the flood came upon the earth."
7.10.
7 days of flood: In the Bible,
Genesis 7:14,
"For in seven days I will send rain on the earth
for forty days and forty nights;
and every living thing that I have made
I will blot out from the face of the ground."

Waiting for the 7th day: In the Babylonian Epic of Gilgamesh, line
146, we read:
"And Utnapishtim, upon the seventh day."
In the Bible, Genesis 8:10, we read,
"He (Noah) waited another seven days..."

Sealing the door and cover of the boat with pitch:

In the Babylonian Atrahasis, we read,
"He (Utnapishtim) brought pitch to seal the door."

In the Bible, Genesis 6:14,
"Make yourself an ark of cypress wood;
make rooms in the ark, and cover it
inside and out with pitch."

The body of Utnapishtim's boat and Noah's Ark (The chassis if you want) were coated (Covered, painted, sealed) with the same material. It is called "Pitch". The Biblical ark of Noah was coated with pitch and tar.
The Babylonian boat was coated (Sealed) with pitch and bitumen, basically and essential the same coating. Bitumen and tar were the very same material in ancient times. The Mesopotamian tablet: The ship of Utnapishtim was sealed with tar (Bitumen).
In the Bible: The boat (Ark) of Noah was sealed with tar.

Making a roof (Cover for the boat): In the Babylonian Atrahasis, we read:
"Make a roof (Cover) over the boat like the Apsu."

In the Bible, Genesis 6:14,
"Make yourself an ark of cypress wood;
make rooms in the ark, and cover it
inside and out with pitch."

In the Bible, Genesis 6:16,
"Make a roof for the ark, and finish it
to a cubit above; and put the door of the ark
in its side; make it with lower, second,
and third decks."

The covenant: In the Babylonian Epic of Gilgamesh, line 165, we read,
"I (Utnapishtim) will remember those days,
and I will never forget them."

In the Bible, Genesis 6:18,
"But I will establish my covenant with you;

and you shall come into the ark,
you, your sons, your wife, and
your sons' wives with you."

In the Bible, Chapter 9, Genesis 9:9, we read,
"As for me, I am establishing my covenant with you
and your descendants after you."

Chapter 9, Genesis 9:10,
"And with every living creature that is with you,
the birds, the domestic animals,
and every animal of the earth with you,
as many as came out of the ark."

Chapter 9, Genesis 9:11,
"I establish my covenant with you,
that never again shall all flesh be cut off
by the waters of a flood,
and never again shall there be
a flood to destroy the earth."

Chapter 9, Genesis 9:12,
"God said, This is the sign of the covenant
that I make between me and
you and every living creature that is with you,
for all future generations."

Offerings and sacrifices: In the Babylonian Epic of Gilgamesh,
lines 156 and 160, we read:
"I (Utnapishtim) sacrificed offerings
and I burned incense,
and the gods smelled the odor
and were pleased."

The Mesopotamian tablet: Lines 156-161:
Utnapishtim made an offering
to the gods on the mountain,
which pleased them enormously.

In a Babylonian-Assyrian version of the story of the flood, Ziusudra sacrificed an ox and a sheep to the gods.
In the Bible, Noah made a sacrifice to god Yahweh.

Chapter 8, Genesis 8:20,
"Then Noah built an altar to the Lord,
and took of every clean animal
and of every clean bird,
and offered burnt offerings on the altar."

In the Bible, Genesis 8:21, we read,
"And when the Lord smelled the pleasing odor..."

The blessing of Utnapishtim and Noah:
The Mesopotamian tablet: Lines 178-188:
"God Enlil went aboard the ship
and blessed Utnapishtim and his wife."

In the Babylonian Epic of Gilgamesh, line 201, we read,
"He (god) blessed us."

In the Bible, god Yahweh too blessed Noah and his family.
In the Bible, Genesis 9:1,
"God blessed Noah and his sons,
and said to them, Be fruitful and multiply,
and fill the earth."

Chapter 9, Genesis 9:7,
"And you, be fruitful and multiply,
abound on the earth and multiply in it."

*** *** ***

Characteristics and dissimilarities of the three Babylonian versions of the story of the flood, the Epic of Gilgamesh and Berossus' account:
The Babylonian stories of the flood shared some resemblance with the Epic of Gilgamesh.
But the clay tablets from Ashurbanipal's library in Nineveh originated at a much later period.

A second (newer) Assyrian story of the flood differs from the Epic of Gilgamesh. In the first and earlier version, Utnapishtim was the main character.

In a newer version, Atrahasis became the leading character. Utnapishtim of the Gilgamesh Epic, in lines 54 to 79 appeared to be a seasoned ship-builder.
In the second Assyrian version, in lines 11 to 17, Atrahasis was depicted as an inexperienced ship-builder, and begged god Ea to draw a design of the boat, so he could build one.
In the first and earliest version of the story of the flood: (First Dynasty of Babylon, circa 1844-1505 B.C.), the larger animals and birds were to be saved, and brought to the boat. The gods asked Utnapishtim to give a name to the boat which would save him and his family.

In the second Babylonian story of the Flood, written or copied in the 11th year of the reign of King Ammisaduqa, when he rebuilt Dur-Ammi-saduqa, the main character is Atramhasis and not Atrahasis.
Atrahasis built a ship but left behind all his possessions.
Worth mentioning here that Atramhasis is an Old Babylonian form for the later Assyrian Atrahasis. In one version of the story, Ziusudra was saved in a boat during the deluge, which lasted seven days. When Ziusudra opened the roof's cover, Utu the sun god appeared to him. After he sacrificed an ox and a sheep, and bowed before Enlil and Anu, Ziusudra received the gift of immortality in Dilmun (Modern day Bahrain).

The Sumerian story of the flood according to Berossus, a priest of the cult of Marduk in Babylon:
Around 275 B.C., Berossus, a contemporary of the king Antiochus I Soter (281-260), wrote in Greek a history of Babylon titled "Babyloniaca".

Unfortunately, his book was lost.
However, few passages from the book were quoted by:
- a-Georgius Syncellus (circa A.D. 792 A.D.),
- b-Eusebius of Caesarea (A.D. 265-340 A.D.),
- c-Flavius Josephus 37-103 A.D.),

- d-King Juba of Mauretania (circa 50 B.C.-23 A.D.),
- e-Alexander Polyhistor (circa 88 B.C.),
- f-Apollodorus of Athens (circa 144 B.C.)

Berossus' story of the flood remained the only and first Babylonian account of the deluge, before the cuneiform clay tablets of Nineveh were discovered. In his story, one of the gods warned Xisuthros of the Flood, and instructed him to build a boat to save his lfe, his family and friends, and animals.
After the flood, Xisuthros disembarked on a mountain in Armenia. And the gods granted him immortality, and joined the gods.
Worth noting that the names of Ziusudra and Xisuthros appeared both in the account of Berossus and in the Sumerian clay tablet of the flood.

The Babylonian story of the Flood and the Biblical account of the Deluge were mentioned on a tablet from Ugarit:
In 1960, Jean Nougayrol announced to the world, the discovery of a fragment of an Ugaritic tablet mentioning the Mesopotamian flood. It contained twenty lines and started with the following:
"When the gods counseled together,
the flood came to the countries."
The remaining 18 lines were similar to passages from Tablet XI (7th century B.C.) of the Babylonian Assyrian version from the library of Ashurbanipal found in Nineveh however a few sections differed from the Ugaritic tablet; here are some examples:
In The Assyro-Babylonian version, Utnapishtim (The Hebrew Noah) is listening to god Ea, from his house in Shuruppak. Ea told Utnapishtim about the Flood.
In the Ugaritic tablet, Utnapishtim was not at home, but in the temple of god Ea who promised to save him and to grant him immortality.
However, what Ea told Utnapishtim in the Assyro-Babylonian version is similar to to what it was recorded on the Ugaritic fragmented tablet, and began in this manner: "Wall, hear!"

Attacking Earth, UFOs: A synopsis of alien invasion of Earth versus German (Remnants of Nazi Germany) UFOs attacks on Earth was entertained and carefully observed by the military and civilian scientists. Herewith excerpts from the synopsis:

178

The difference between an alien invasion and German UFOs' attacks: There is an enormous difference between an alien invasion of Earth, and German UFOs' attack on Earth.
Grosso modo, the difference could be explained as follows (Briefly):

I-Should the aliens decide to attack Earth.
a-What the aliens or extraterrestrials would not do:
1-Contrary to what it has been said and depicted in movies, the aliens or extraterrestrials would not station their mothership over Earth and block the sun. The mothership will not stand still over New York or Washington, DC, and let our jets and missiles aim at it. *Au contraire,* the mothership will remain beyond Earth's orbit, and/or very far away from Earth and our site.
And no satellite, no radar or any detection system known to mankind will ever detect and register its location, simply because it is not a conventional flying machine, but a time-machine, or more precisely a time-space-pockets' machine.
2-They will not lower down gigantic robots with funny looking heads and bizarre mechanical bodies to roam our streets and avenues, walk over cars, and smash buildings with their iron or steel toes, and in the process destroy all objects and life-forms on Earth.
They have invaded Earth for purposes that should be protected and accomplished by preserving Earth, and not by destroying it, otherwise, they would have defeated their own agenda and objectives. Such purposes could be harvesting and collecting Earth's resources, and destroying these resources would be a blow to their invasion.
3-They would not exchange fire with United States army, ground forces and air force. Simply because they would not use "fire".
Instead they will deploy galactic weapons and weather-weapons systems beyond our imagination and comprehension.
4-They would not send robots/mechanical/machines-creatures to houses and buildings' basements searching for those who shot at them or are hiding underground.

b-What the aliens or extraterrestrials would or could do:
There are lots of incomprehensive things, the aliens could do to us. The list is endless.

179

But just to name a few:

- 1-They could/would suck up the oxygen in the air, and we will suffocate in minutes or seconds.
- 2-They could/would shift Earth' axe, and as you already know, Earth's fate will be sealed.
- 3-They could/would surround Earth with their "Plasma-Anti Matter Belt".
- 4-They could/would incapacitate us physically, all of us in seconds.
- 5-They could/would alter our genes, DNA, molecules, cells and the very structure of our organism, body, etc.
- 6-They could/would use the "Compressor" (the "Black-Conic-Box Weapon System-BCB) that evaporates, transposes, transports and moves cities and continents from one place to another.

Nota bene: B.C.B is an acronym for the infamous Black Conic Box, also called "Compressor". It was reported that the United States military is currently working on phase one of an exotic weapon system known as the BCB. Testing is done at AUTEC, an American military naval base in the Bahamas.

Insiders and scientists nickname the program, or the "gadget" the "Compressor". The gadget consists of a small black cylindrical container, 1 foot in height by ½ foot in width.
"It is a movable (Mobile) device that functions without an external source of energy" claimed a foreign scientist working for the military on an anti-gravity-electro-magnetic project, based on quantum physics. In other words, it works without an electric current, batteries, or any similar source of power.
It is neither electronic nor atomic. It is programmable and re-programmable. It draws its energy from within.
An internal cell located in the very inner circle of the cone emits an enormous amount of "sucking power" capable of absorbing, transporting, resizing, and condensing a large amount of contents and materials into the cone.
"The 'sucked up' materials can be anything, all sorts of things...the box can suck up everything you have in your apartment, absolutely everything, chairs, tables, furniture, your bed, your closets, your

clothes and even your pets, melt them like ice-cream and boom, shoot them right in the box..." said a well-informed insider, who allegedly works at AUTEC, where pertinent experiments are conducted.

It was heard from the grapevine, that the "Sucking Power" of this device has the capability of de-fragmenting any object, and reducing it to any desirable size, density, format and weight.
This is based upon the fact, that everything in the universe is made out of molecules, and the density of the molecules dictates the nature, weight and size of any object, any substance, any matter in the world.
By reducing, decreasing, increasing and/or altering the properties of molecules, any object can be reduced and/or enlarged either to the biggest or smallest desired shape, and consequently be transported to any destination, regardless of space and distance.
The process can also de-fragment the molecules to a certain point, where the biggest object can fit inside the smallest possible container.

Some have claimed that this or a similar "Sucking Technology" device was responsible for the vanishing and/or disappearance of many ships and airplanes in the Bermuda Triangle.
A French-American scientist who vaguely described the black box (Sucking Device) stated verbatim, word for word, "Only those anomalies of the Bermuda Triangle that have occurred after September 1958 were unintentionally caused by extraterrestrials-US joint programs.
The government is not so vicious to cause all these tragedies.
In the first phase of their operation, they (United States) needed some adjustments; they did not know how to regulate the equilibrium and the opening (Sliding and Bumping) of the "Tectonic Vacuum".
It is not exactly a tectonic vacuum, but pretty close."
The BCB can suck up your whole life, everything you know, everything you are thinking about, your thoughts, your ideas, your health, your memory, your brain, and store them in the conic box. They can easily reprogram you, and send back information and disinformation to disillusion your brain and screw up your life."

The insider went on to say: "The BCB can destroy or confuse a person's ATP (Adenosine Triphosphate), which is the energy coin of the cell. When cells are destroyed, molecules and membranes die.

The "Sucking Machine" de-regulates the transfer of energy and all sources of vitality from chemical bonds to your body absorbing energy called Endergonic, and causes destructive reactions in the cell." When asked to elaborate further, he replied calmly, "I don't want to end up like Bender!"

- 7-They could/would incapacitate our mental faculties, erase our memory, freeze us in time, etc...in this context, the BCB becomes extremely effective, because it can also be used as a "mental weapon". It controls everything in your mind and in your body. It creates new habits, and makes you addicted to "something you don't want in your life".

Nota bene: Because it empties your brain from all its contents, and put in (in your brain) new things, new information, new habits, new desires and new thoughts, the person who is operating the machine becomes your master. He is in charge now, and you become his puppet. It controls your dopamine.

Dopamine is an important neurotransmitter (messenger) in the brain. Science defined Dopamine "as a catecholamine (a class of molecules that serve as neurotransmitters and hormones.)

The BCB is more than a military weapon..." explained a former military scientist who worked on mind control programs, sponsored by governmental agencies.

He added, "In the past, and for many years, the government tried unsuccessfully to understand how this horrible alien technology worked.

The extraterrestrial scientists who were working with military astrophysicists in secret underground military labs/installations demonstrated to us how this machine works. But none could really understand what made it work.

- 8-They coul disable all our communications systems and satellites, including radios, TV transmissions, Internet, military and industrial information and communications' channels.

- 9- They could/would neutralize all our weapons systems, military bases, missiles, submarines, defense facilities, etc.
- 10-They could/would shut off electricity and all our sources of energy, all over the world.
- 11-They could/would shower Earth with germs, bacteria and diseases, and wipe out the entire human race.
- 12-They can hit us from outer space and from multiple galactic/space locations, we can never reach or destroy with our current technology.
- 13-They could/would alter our ecological system; create apocalyptic tsunamis, earthquakes and unstoppable volcanoes' eruptions around the globe.
- 14-They could/would eliminate Earth's ozone layer, nullify Earth's protection shield, and expose Earth to the deadly cosmic radiations.
- 15-They could/would interfere with Earth's gravity, and make the Earth spin in all directions, and its inhabitants (humans and animals) and all objects float in the air like feathers.
- 16-They could/would electrocute everything in our waters (oceans, seas, rivers, lakes, reservoirs).
- 17-They could/would burn us alive with their "Death-Beams", simply by redirecting and intensifying the solar rays and energy; they will reduce us to ashes.
- 18-They could/would take us back in time and space, and dump us in the infinite void.
- 19-They could/would hit us and pulverize us from their own planet (s), without flying one inch.
- 20-They could/would shoot down every single missile and jet we have at our disposals, and destroy all the jet carriers and nuclear submarines of all nations in minutes.

The list is endless.

Thus a direct confrontation with aliens/extraterrestrials will never occur, as you usually see in movies.

Nota bene: We are not referring to the Intraterrestrial Aliens who co-inhabit Earth.

II-Should the German New World Order UFOs and their scientists decide to attack us:
The German UFOs' tactics, techniques and attacks would be very different, and similar to a certain degree, simply because the Nazi New World Order has a totally different agenda. They are not seeking the total annihilation of Earth, *au contraire,* they want to preserve a major part of it, so they would/could dominate what's left from Earth, and control every aspect of our life.
The German UFOs are capable of so many catastrophic things, to name a few:

- 1-They could disable all our communications systems and satellites, including radios, TV transmissions, Internet, military and industrial information and communications' channels.
- 2-They could neutralize all our weapons systems, military bases, missiles, submarines, defense facilities, etc.
- 3-They could/would shoot down every single missile and jet we have at our disposals, and destroy all the jet carriers and nuclear submarines of all nations in minutes.
- 4-They could shut off electricity and all our sources of energy, all over the world.
- 5-They can hit us from outer space and multiple galactic/space locations, we can never reach or destroy with our current technology.
- 6-They could alter our ecological system, change Earth's weather and climate, create apocalyptic tsunamis, earthquakes and unstoppable volcanoes' eruptions around the globe.
- 7-They could electrocute everything in our waters (oceans, seas, rivers, lakes, reservoirs).
- 8-They could/would use the "Black Liquid" which was described in the Aliens Transcripts (AT). I have written about the "Black Liquid" in my previous books; here is an excerpt about the Final Stage of an attack:

From the bottom of the spaceships, a special substance will be diffused, and will land in huge, swirling streams.
It is a black liquid, mixed with light and electricity, and some strange sparkling particles, which is a form of energy or radiation.

It smells like fire and brimstone, but strangely, it is cold to the touch. Yet, it burns everything that touches it. This is a tool of annihilation, a tool that no one can fight.

The substance slithers inexorably over the ground, the buildings, and the stranded cars like icy cold lava waves. It sweeps away many people, killing them instantly. Once it covers a large area, it begins to coagulate, expand and rise up, foot by foot, until it reaches the height of the tallest building on Earth. Slowly, it will harden, and solidify itself into steel-like state.

Huge stacks of smoke will rise up into the sky, cars will melt, buildings will collapse, and fires start everywhere, seemingly not only by the touch of the substance, but spontaneously, when the wind carries the particles of energy into flammable materials. The combination of images and sounds will be that of chaos, pain, confusion, total destruction and death.

The fire and brimstone smell mix with that of burning flesh and of melting metal, plastic and rubber. Then, all of a sudden, the substance stops growing, and assumes the appearance of craggy mountains, with sharp edges and canyons.

A very few who had survived, but had nowhere to go to, now tried to climb on the substance, since the earth itself was buried in it. This was futile, since the substance was too slippery for the climb. They started to fall and slip, and were instantly killed. These conditions will continue over the entire world for two days; no one will be left alive on the scorched Earth..."

- 9-The Nazi New World Order scientists and their UFOs could/would use weapons systems capable of holographic zooming, and slowing down time, or prolonging it indefinitely; this was discussed by our military scientists.

Imagine people accustomed to working from 9 am to 5 pm, going to work in the morning to a day that seemingly never ends.

Or an ambulance with a patient that needs emergency treatment never seeming to reach the nearest hospital. What should be a five or ten minute ambulance ride takes five weeks to travel the same distance in normal time. Obviously the patient will expire, and the 9 to 5 employee will collapse and die from complete physical exhaustion. What seems to be going on here, is that the physical body is straining under the conditions of the slowing down of time, that the mind seems to be completely unaware of.

185

Imagine the scenario seen by people on the ground, of airplanes dropping like stones out of the sky, due to the fact that they have run out of fuel before ever reaching their destination.
On the pilot's instruments, everything has slowed down except for the fuel consumption by the plane's engines.

The stewardesses have run out of food and drink in the galleys, due to the indeterminable length of the flight, and ask the pilot and co-pilot why they have run out before the plane has landed, when they knew they were sufficiently stocked before the flight took off. This particular flight from Washington D.C. to New York City, which normally takes only 50 minutes, has been airborne for a month.

Here is another another frightening example of a passenger onboard this flight, having an urgent need to go to the bathroom, taking up to a week to unzip and pull down his pants!
What then would happen to the rest of the world, and people's daily lives? Work schedules and appointments, food and medical supply deliveries, nuclear plants that generate electricity needing maintenance, and nuclear warheads needing fuses and detonators to have scheduled maintenance and replacement?

Or picture a parent going to pick up their kids after school, and taking what seems forever to reach them. Or a woman going into labor but never delivering the baby? She will be in labor for ever.

Is there any way to solve this problem?
Unfortunately, there is no way to solve this problem, as the mind has no way of becoming aware of what is happening, or realizing what to do about it.
The purpose of such a weapons system is to completely break down the fabric of society, and incapacitate all faculties and tools of humans, to defend themselves against the Nazi New World Order (NNWO) and/or aliens' attacks.
By how much is time is slowed down, and is there any way to quantify or measure the rate of the slowing down of time?
The NNWO, the Lyrans, the Dracos (from Alpha Draconis), the Zeta Reticulans and the Anunnaki, as well as other civilizations

186

from the Ashtari (Adelbaran) constellations have this weapons system and can slow time down 100 percent, to the point where time particles begin to disintegrate, and an entire race of beings can be transported back in time. It was reported that the Nazi scientists and their occult societies which were in direct contacts with aliens have already mastered this weapons system. And it is frightening.

Project Omega:
There was a "Project Omega", which remains completely unknown to this day to any Ufologist, which dealt with this technology. In 1957 and 1958, the Gray aliens told President Dwight Eisenhower about this technology.
The American military and President Eisenhower did not believe it is possible, until the Grays "rewound the tape of time" to the point where they were able to not only see a holographic projection of Jesus, but listen to his voice as well.

The Grays, General Marshall, President Eisenhower, and D-Day.

General Marshall was present at this meeting, and decided to ask the Grays if they could re-project an event that occurred in World War II, known only to General Omar Bradley, General Patton, General Eisenhower and himself. He gave them the date and location of this event, and waited for the holographic projection. What they then saw before them, was accurate down to the very last detail. The Grays then went even one step further to reveal two letters within the holographic projection: One, a speech to be given by Eisenhower in the event of a successful storming of the beaches of Normandy on D-Day, and another speech to be given, in the event that this D-Day event was a failure. The existence and contents of the two letters were known only to Generals Bradley and Eisenhower. Also shown were the six draft letters written by Eisenhower and his secretary.

The device used to create a holographic projection.
"What is the device used to create this holographic projection system that can show past, present and future events in time?"

187

It is called the Miraya."
Many extraterrestrial civilizations have this technology.

HZ: An acronym for Holographic Zooming.
From talking to a European scientist who is allegedly working on reverse-engineering the alien's or the German "HZ", the following was obtained, verbatim, "Holography as applied in the project means the projection of a picture or a substance that has been de-fragmented and transported via a grid. It is similar to what you see reflected in a mirror. However, it is more realistic, because it interacts with you, and can be programmed and reprogrammed.
In other words and simply put, you take anything you want, a tank, a building, a car, a whole city and you create the tank, the building, a city, in a sequence of numbers (ones and zeros).
The sequence has its own language and frequency.
The language is used for command.
The sequence is used for programming. In doing so, you will be able to know what constitutes the substance and "inertia" of everything in the world. And inertia has also its one substance. And the substance itself can be broken like an atom. Much more, you can divide the inertia into molecules. Each molecule will have its own sequence, like a DNA. By doing so, you can change and/or totally alter its nature. For example, you take the Empire State Building. You enter its blueprints into the grid.
The grid will read its sequence which was created through the re-programming using the code of ones and zeros. At distance, and without even touching the Empire State Building, you can disintegrate it, erase it, and destroyed...you wiped it from the face of the earth by a simple holographic process.
Another fascinating characteristic is the creation of something that does not exist at all. For instance, you can create a whole city with the holographic grid, and project it on a huge scale, big, as big as a small city. On your grid, it is a virtual image. But on a landscape, it is a reality. Mind you, it is not an alternate reality. It is not a camouflage. It is real. This technique can be used to deceive the enemy, and of course to confuse everybody.
You can transport New York from its actual location to another, and substitute or replace it with the holographic projection you have created."

188

The measurements of genome/DNA chips of any substance, and pertinent holographic reconstruction have enormous military applications. It is difficult to understand how extraterrestrials and some Nazi scientists manage to do this. Scientists have already done something with these measurements, but in a different area. They call it "microarray measurements."

- 10-The Nazi New World Order scientists and their UFOs could/would use the "D.S.I."

A French-American scientist who claims to be one of the "brains" working on D. S. I., stated (As is, word for word and unedited): "D. S. I. makes things disappear without leaving behind any trace or evidence. It is a formidable source and tool of energy that cannot be detected; a sort of plasma-gas bubbles vortex that can suck up ships and planes and make them vanish. We have seen these phenomena when German and unidentified spacecrafts not from this world appeared over the Bermuda Triangle. " Asking him, "Is it similar to those notorious rising methane bubbles?"

He laughed, and said: "Yes, on the surface, (For lack of proper wording) but it is more complicated and more destructive than you can imagine. Don't ask me how the system works. But one thing I can tell you, the energy comes from the bottom of the sea or some hidden areas serving as a temporary base for UFOs. You know, D. S. I. can open a wide section deep down in the ocean and create a vortex-vacuum capable of swallowing a 85,000 tons ship, in matter of seconds! The ship goes down instantly, and dissipates inside the 'Hollow-Opening"!!

Are we ready to fight back the UFOs?
NO! And this is one of the paramount reasons, our governments would not admit the reality, existence and threats of UFOs. So let's move on.

The New Wonder-Weapons of the Nazi New World Order.

Those flying machines you see in the skies are not extraterrestrial or American-made. They are German UFOs which can destroy the world in minutes, to name a few:

189

1-Die Mutterschiff Einsatzkommando. S1 & S2 (The Mothership, also called The mother-ship Striking Force. It flew over many areas in the United States, including Arizona, Texas, Nevada)
2-Neuer Bestellugsstrom (New Order Stream)
3-Schwarzer Wind (Black-Wind. It flew over Belgium, Brazil, Mexico and the United States)
4-Deutsche Tornado-Wut (German-Tornado Fury. It flew over Brazil, Belgium, Mexico, Chile, Peru, The Bahamas, Bermuda Triangle area, the United States.)
5-Mehrlagige Kuppel (The Multi-layered cupola. It flew over Russia, Poland, Holland, the United States.)
6-Die Schwerkraft Aufhebemaschine. (The XV1 Anti-Gravity Sphere Machine. It flew over Mexico, Chile, The Bahamas, Bermuda Triangle area, the United States)
7-Jenseitsflugmaschine (Version V-12)
8-Die Glocke (Version UV3)

Nota Bene: The Vril, Geist 7, the Haunebu's first 7 types, the RFZ 1 (Rundflugzeug 1), the Reichsflugscheiben or Hauneburg-Geräte, The Foo Fighters and other types of German UFOs are now a relic from the past by German standard.
Consequently, they are no longer in the arsenal inventory of the Nazi New World Order.
What we are currently seeing in our skies is: German Nazi challenge, harassment, intimidation and an Ultimatum. And there is nothing we can do about it, except seeking shelter.
And let me repeat one more what I have said previously: We must right away start building underground cities, as Switzerland did, long time ago.

No country on Earth is safe from this apocalyptic annihilation except...

No country on Earth is safe from this apocalyptic annihilation except Canada, Argentina, The Vatican City, Spain, Austria, Antarctica, Portugal, the Bahamas' area, and a few Latin and Middle/Near Eastern countries, including Palestine/Israel. (The New German World Order considers Israel as an Arab state, so no reason to destroy Israel!)

We should unite, we should forget our differences, we should stop hating and discrediting each other and join our efforts (individuals, nations and governments) as one universal family to face the forthcoming global catastrophe, which some alert and bright minds have already called: World War Three. We might succeed! We must!!

And for a while, I laughed at the "Apocalyptic man" with a bright mind who predicted UFOs' WWIII.

And he replied, "People laughed too at Noah as he commenced to build his boat in the middle of an arid land."

The German NNWO's UFOs must be mind-blowing spacecrafts in order to bring apocalypse on Earth?

Are they entirely German or the results of cooperation with aliens?

And how much do we know about their striking force?

Answer:

There are several types and classes of German UFOs which stretch over a period of almost 85 years. The general public and ufologists are to a certain degree familiar with the first types of German UFOs which were either produced or designed during WWII, such as the:

Arado-Brandenburg's Geist Vril 7,

The Jenseitsflugmaschine,

Die Glocke,

Rundflugzeug RFZ-1 to 7,

Haunebu, etc.

Even though, they were the prototype of forthcoming magnificent machines, and considered to be archaic by NNWO's new technological/scientific standards, these machines can wipe out all the crafts and jets we have at our disposal, in matter of hours. Those UFOs are no longer in use.

The German UFOs/USOs which were mass-produced between 1946 and 1958 are more sophisticated and deadlier, yet the high command of the NNWO removed them from their inventory, and were replaced by the most formidable and destructive UFOs of all time, such as Die Mutterschiff Einsatzkommando, S1 & S2 types, which is the "Mothership", and the ultimate striking force of NNWO which flew over many areas in the United States, including Arizona, Texas, and Nevada.

191

The triangular spacecraft, the Schwarzer Wind, which flew over Belgium, Brazil, Mexico and the United States, and the multi-acrobatic series of all, the Die Schwerkraft Aufhebemaschine, which flew over Mexico, Chile Argentina, The Bahamas, Bermuda Triangle area, and the United States.

And of course, the super heavy one, the Jenseitsflugmaschine, Version V-12. To compare a WWII UFO to Die Mutterschiff Einsatzkommando, to Die Schwerkraft Aufhebemaschine, or to the Mehrlagige Kuppel, which flew over Russia, Poland, Holland, Belgium, and the United States, is like comparing a Ford T Model to a Concorde.

Their striking force is beyond our comprehension.

They can wipe out the entire United States and Russia air forces in minutes. We don't know much about their mode of operation and technical specifications and characteristics.

Years ago, the American administration compiled extensive files on the earliest types of Germany UFOs.

Few had access to those files. In addition to the top brass at the Pentagon, the USAF, and the elite of German scientists we have recruited during 2 years, few presidents, presidential advisors and scientists were able to construct an idea about the striking force, capabilities and flight mysteries of those spacecrafts, to name a few, President Richard Nixon, President George Bush Sr., Allen Welsh Dulles, Richard Helms, Dr. Dennis Gabor, Dr. Edward Teller, John R. Steelman, Dr. James B. Conant, Dr. Vannevar Bush, and of course Bob Haldeman, President Nixon's Chief of Staff, who was introduced to the world of UFOs by General Robert Landry, President Truman's Air Force Aide

Au, Aw, Awu: Ancient Hebrew: It corresponds to the Akkadian and Sumerian "Ya".

From Ya, the Hebrew words Yah or Jah derived, and were used as prefix for Yahweh.

"A", the Babylonian, Sumerian and Assyrian deity often referred to as Aê, and Ea was represented by and identified as Au, Ya'u /Ya which is a variation of Ea, an ancient Babylonian deity.

Ya corresponds to the Hebrew Au, Aw, Awu.

Aurora airship crash in Texas, April 17, 1897, the:
The first recorded event of a UFO sighting in the United States goes back to 1897, which took place in Aurora, Texas.
The Aurora sighting does not mean that UFOs were not spotted during that phase/era in other parts of the world, and/or in other regions of the United States. For we know that numerous sightings occurred in Europe, Brazil, Africa, and the Middle East.
But bear in mind that the year 1896 marks only the beginning of the American UFOs' saga which was later exaggerated and embellished by ufologists and ill-informed ancient astronauts' theorists.

Here is an excerpt from the Dallas Morning News, April 19, 1897:
About 6 o'clock this morning the early risers of Aurora were astonished at the sudden appearance of the airship which has been sailing throughout the country.
It was traveling due north, and much nearer the earth than before. Evidently some of the machinery was out of order, for it was making a speed of only ten or twelve miles an hour, and gradually settling toward earth. It sailed over the public square and when it reached the north part of town it collided with the tower of Judge Proctor's windmill and went to pieces with a terrific explosion, scattering debris over several acres of ground, wrecking the windmill and water tank and destroying the judge's flower garden. The pilot of the ship is supposed to have been the only one aboard, and while his remains are badly disfigured, enough of the original has been picked up to show that he was not an inhabitant of this world. Mr. T. J. Weems, the U.S. Signal Service officer at this place and an authority on astronomy, gives it as his opinion that the pilot was a native of the planet Mars. Papers found on his person-evidently the records of his travels are written in some unknown hieroglyphics, and cannot be deciphered.

This ship was too badly wrecked to form any conclusion as to its construction or motive power. It was built of an unknown metal, resembling somewhat a mixture of aluminium and silver, and it must have weighed several tons. The town today is full of people who are viewing the wreckage and gathering specimens of strange metal from the debris. The pilot's funeral will take place at noon tomorrow."

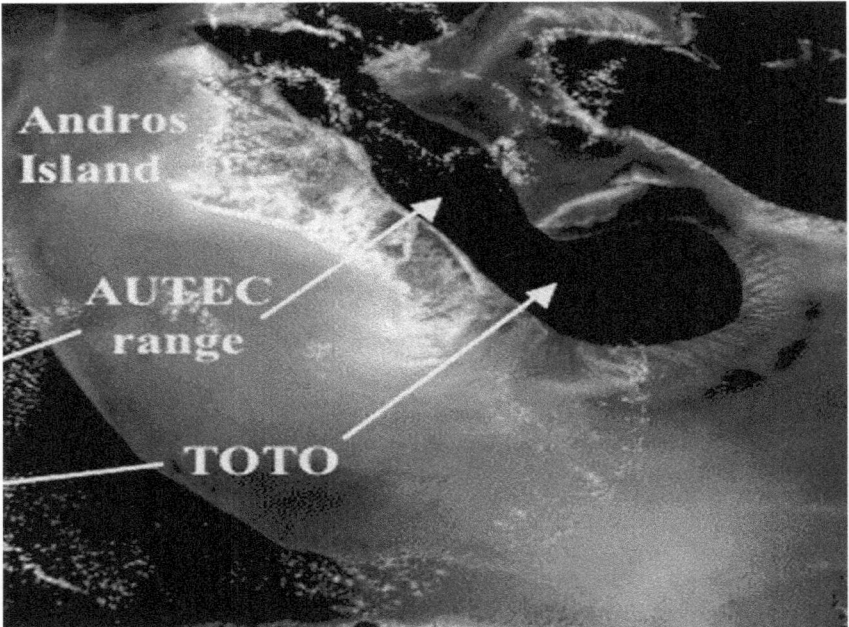

AUTEC facility, Andros Island.
AUTEC/TOTO. A satellite view by NASA.

AUTEC: Acronym for Atlantic Undersea Test and Evaluation Center.
Sophisticated and Exotic Aliens' Weapons Systems at AUTEC.
I. Introduction
II. Weapons systems out of this world
1- HZP: An acronym for Holographic Zooming Project
2- Earth-made holographic zooming
a- Refractive Components
b- Reflective Components
c- Diffractive Components
3- Extraterrestrials-made holographic zooming

194

I. Introduction:

Numerous ufologists have suggested that the aliens and the United States government are working together on very sophisticated and exotic weapons systems at AUTEC.

These claims were never substantiated, or proven factual.

For obvious reasons, none of the ufologists and conspiracy theorists was able to make a solid case out of their claims and arguments. In addition, none of them had access to any document, documentation, evidence, and/or military witnesses, or civilian scientists from the naval base, as they have aggressively claimed in the past, when they argued and presented their Roswell and Area 51 scenarios.

However, it appeared that some "insiders" managed to learn about Top Secret weapons projects and programs allegedly, jointly carried and executed by an alien race and the military.

In the United States, a history Channel program called UFO Hunters hosted by the very distinguished Dr. Bill Birnes, publisher of UFO magazine, and a highly respected author and scholar referred to these aliens-US programs in one of the episodes on USOs and AUTEC.

I was one of the guests who discussed at length the AUTEC subject, and its involvement in said projects. I provided explosive information, but everything I have said about these programs never made it to the small screen. My statements were deleted or censored/removed.

II. Weapons systems out of this world:

Based upon some unsubstantiated, by assumed highly reliable accounts by military scientists and leaks from AUTEC's high profile employees, the following has been established:

1- HZP: An acronym for Holographic Zooming Project.

A prototype is en route.

195

AUTEC

The second prototype will be available in 2010.
The previous project was traditional; meaning based upon known scientific data, and is described as follows:

2-Earth-made holographic zooming:
This prototype system, Holographic Zoom Lens HZL-C-1000, represents the first hardware version of a stepwise holographic zoom lens described by B.D. Guenther and C. D. Leonard in Technical Report, T-79-12 for the U.S. Army Missile Research and Development Command, 1978.
As stated in that report, optical components may be classified into the following three groups according to the mechanism by which they operate.
- a-Refractive Components
- b- Reflective Components

196

- c- Diffractive Components

3- Extraterrestrials-made holographic zooming:
The extraterrestrial holographic zooming is quite different, and much more complex, complicated and superior.
The extraterrestrial holographic zooming is quite different, and much more complex, complicated and superior.
Data and technical specs are kept secret.
However, from talking to a European scientist who is allegedly working on this project with the extraterrestrials, the following was obtained. The scientist said verbatim, word for word, as is, and unedited: "Holography as applied in the project means the projection of a picture or a substance that has been de-fragmented and transported via a grid. It is similar to what you see reflected in a mirror. However, it is more realistic, because it interacts with you, and can be programmed and reprogrammed.

In other words and simply put, you take anything you want, a tank, a building, a car, a whole city and you create the tank, the building, a city, in a sequence of numbers (ones and zeros).
The sequence has its own language and frequency.
The language is used for command.
The sequence is used for programming. In doing so, you will be able to know what constitutes the substance and "inertia" of everything in the world. And inertia has also its one substance. And the substance itself can be broken like an atom.
Much more, you can divide the inertia into molecules. Each molecule will have its own sequence, like a DNA. By doing so, you can change and/or totally alter its nature. For example, you take the Empire State Building. You enter its blueprints into the grid. The grid will read its sequence which was created through the re-programming using the code of ones and zeros.
At distance, and without even touching the Empire State Building, you can disintegrate it, erase it, and destroyed...you wiped it from the face of the earth by a simple holographic process.
Another fascinating characteristic is the creation of something that does not exist at all.
For instance, you can create a whole city with the holographic grid, and project it on a huge scale, big, as big as a small city.

On your grid, it is a virtual image. But on a landscape, it is a reality. Mind you, it is not an alternate reality. It is not a camouflage. It is real.

This technique can be used to deceive the enemy, and of course to confuse everybody.

You can transport New York from its actual location to another, and substitute or replace it with the holographic projection you have created."

The measurements of genome/DNA chips of any substance, and pertinent holographic reconstruction have enormous military applications. It is difficult to understand how extraterrestrials manage to do this. Scientists have already done something with these measurements, but in a different area.

They call it "microarray measurements."

III. Holographic zooming going on at some intelligence agencies:

There is something close to holographic zooming going on at some intelligence agencies, and in the labs of avant garde research companies. By comparison to the extraterrestrials' technique it is rudimentary, but the potentials and future developments are enormous.

David Crane said: "There's no doubt that geospatial information systems (GIS) have become an important component of network centric warfare (a.k.a. net-centric warfare).

Military analysts and strategists, as well as those tasked with Homeland Security missions, have to be able to visualize geographic areas and correlate those pictures with relevant mission data/information.

Official statement from Northrop Grumman: "In the past, geospatial information, or geospatial intelligence, was displayed and presented in the form of paper maps. Northrop Grumman Mission Systems'ultra-cool Touch table Immersive Collaboration System, billed as "the next step in advanced GIS collaboration", has changed all that.

Now, military and Homeland Security analysts, planners, and strategists can manipulate images in real time, and thus better assimilate the geospatial information and intelligence that's presented.

This will, hopefully, result in faster decisions through a better overall tactical and strategic understanding of the battle-space."

IV. D.S.I: Acronym for Deep Sea Integrated Bubbles Program. It seems likes a meta science fiction story, but the military scientists are vigorously working on the program.

a- D. S. I. and the extraterrestrials:

As a matter of fact, they don't call it anymore program, but system, for it was reported, that D.S.I. is in its final stage.
What is D. S. I.? It is a mystery.
No data or specs are available, because it is beyond top secret. However, it was allegedly reported that D. S. I. is a system created by extraterrestrials, and co-developed by military scientists.
It can sink ships without torpedoes, and shoot down airplanes without missiles. In addition, it can melt anything that sails or flies without leaving any trace!
A French-American scientist who claims to be one of the "brains" working on D. S. I., stated (As is, word for word and unedited): "D. S. I. makes things disappear without leaving behind any trace or evidence. It is a formidable source and tool of energy that cannot be detected; a sort of plasma-gas bubbles vortex that can suck up ships and planes and make them vanish."
Asking him, "Is it similar to those notorious rising methane bubbles?" He laughed, and said: "Yes, on the surface, (For lack of proper wording) but it is more complicated and more destructive than you can imagine. Don't ask me how the system works? But one thing I can tell you, the energy comes from the bottom of the sea. You know, D. S. I. can open a wide section deep down in the ocean and create a vortex-vacuum capable of swallowing a 85,000 tons ship, in matter of seconds! The ship goes down instantly, and dissipates inside the 'Hollow-Opening"!!

b-AUTEC and the Atlantis scenario:

Some ufologists and channelers have claimed that AUTEC is sitting on the top of Atlantis. A so-called medium (Well-known by the way) stated, "Because AUTEC is situated above an opening leading to Atlantis, this ideal position allows AUTEC to make ships and airplanes disappear.

It is happening, we know it..." Those who believe in the prophecies of Edgar Cayce are convinced that the vanishings of ships in the Bermuda Triangle are caused by a source of energy coming from the bottom of the sea, where Atlantis is allegedly located, and/or seems to reappear from time to time. Rationalists and scientists dismiss the whole idea and call it "Ufology nonsense".

However, there is a large group of scientists who entertains the idea, and/or the possibility that a certain kind of gas-bubbles can eventually, and in theory sink a ship. But none attaches this possibility to an extraterrestrial-United States secret program at AUTEC.

V-AUTEC underwater military bases:

These massive underwater military bases look from the surface to be rectangular/traditional compound structures. However upon entering them underwater, they expand in all directions, and are extremely extensive. And all of them are joint human-alien operations.

Starting from the second underwater level, compartments are divided into large operation rooms, separated by elaborate long corridors, curving at 90 degrees every hundred feet or so, with doors that can drop down from the ceiling to seal off segments in the event of radiation leakage, or any matter related to internal security. One of the interesting characteristics of these doors in the corridors is the circular porthole-like windows within what is a whitish metal of extraterrestrial origin.

None of these metallic alloys are possible here due to earth's gravity, and as such have to be done in orbit aboard the Space Shuttle. Interestingly enough, this technology has been shared by American, Russian and Israeli military scientists. At one time British and French scientists complained of being left out of the loop, to which the Americans responded very candidly "We don't trust Europeans – especially the French!" To which the French retorted that they would withhold all information garnered from the Cassini-Huygens mission to Saturn. An American three star general was quick to respond by saying "This is not the first time you Europeans have withheld information from us. Remember the Belgian incident?" (Aurora). The mode of transportation down to the underwater base and within the base is also fascinating.

From the surface, one enters a craft that looks like a silvery metallic spinning top, approximately 8ft in diameter, that can comfortably accommodate four passengers, and corkscrews its way downwards centrifugally around a rod using a form of magnetic propulsion for what seems to be a only a few seconds down to an unknown depth.

The "Spinning Mobile Satellite":
From the second underwater level on down, the "Spinning Mobile Satellite" (SMS) travels horizontally and reaches its final destination at an undisclosed level of the base at which it again dives into water. It is at that level/destination that you will find the habitat and work center of the Grays.
Only the highest level personnel with top clearance can go there. Not even President Barack Obama or Vice-president Joe Biden, or any member of Congress/Senate are allowed access to that level at these facilities. This clearance status was decided upon (jointly) by the NSA, the CIA, the United States Air Force, the DOD and NASA. Even the FBI has been excluded from this exclusive little club.
This is perfectly appropriate, since politicians come and go, whilst the military are sworn to secrecy, the average career of top military brass are thirty or more years, and they take their secrets with them to the grave.
See Russian Aquatic Plasma Corridors.

Authors, thinkers, scientists, investigators, witnesses, dignitaries, and personalities who made an impact on ufology:
A
Ackerman, John B.
Adair, David
Adams, Col. W. A.
Adamski, George
Akdogan Haktan
Aldrich, Jan
Alexander, John
Alvarez, Louis
Amendola, Sal
Anderson, Dennis K.

Andrews, Colin
Andrews, George C.
Andrus, Walter H.
Anka, Darryl
Anthony, Gary
Appelle, Stuart
Arbel, Dr. Ilil
Armstrong, Neil
Arnold, Kenneth
Ashayana, Deane
Asimov, Isaac

B

Bagley, Al
Baker, Robert
Dalducci, Mgr. Corrado
Ballester Olmos, Vicente-Juan
Balthaser, Dennis G.
Bartholic, Barbara
Bassett, Stephen
Bell, Art
Bennett, Colin
Bennewitz, Paul
Berliner, Don
Bernardi, Linda
Bethune, Graham
Bielek, Al
Bigelow, Robert T.
Billingham, John
Birdsall, Graham
Birnbaum, Joel
Birnes Hayfield, Nancy
Birnes, William J.
Bishop Jason
Bishop, Greg
Bloecher, Ted
Blumberg, Baruch
Booth, B. J.

Boras, David
Boulay R. A.
Boylan, Richard J.
Bramley, William
Branton
Bray, Arthur
Brockhouse Smith, Wilbert
Brookesmith, Peter
Brown Townsend, Thomas
Brown, Bob
Brown, Courtney
Bruce, Alexandra "Chica"
Bruni, Georgina
Bryant, Larry
Buggren, Warren
Bullard, Thomas Eddie
Burgess, Woodbury
Burisch, Dan
Burroughs, John
Bush, Vannevar

C
Cameron, Duncan
Cameron, Ed
Cameron, Grant
Campbell, Glen
Cannon, Dolores
Carey, Tom
Carpenter John
Carter, Jimmy, President
Casimira, Trish
Casteel, Sean
Castello, Thomas
Catamas, Scott
Chalker, Bill
Clarke, Arthur C.
Clark, David
Clark, Jerome

Clark, John
Clark. Russell Vernon
Clarke, Arthur C.
Clear, Constance
Coleman, Loren
Colin, Andrews
Collier, Alex
Collins, Tim
Commander X
Condon Edward
Connors, Wendy
Conroy, Ed
Constable Trevor, James
Coonts, Stephen
Cooper, Gordon
Cooper, Milton William
Cooper, Timothy S.
Coppens, Philip
Cornet, Bruce
Corrado, Balducci, Monsignor
Corso, Lt. Colonel Philip
Corum, James F.
Cosnette, Dave
Coy, Gregory
Crystal, Ellie

D

Davids, Paul
Davenport, Peter
Davis, Lisa
De Vere Nicolas
Dean, Robert
Dennis Glenn
Dennis Stacy
Deuley, Thomas P.
DeVore, Edna
Dickinson Terence
Dilettoso Jim
Dolan, Richard

Doty, Richard
Dowden, Russell
Drake, Dr. Frank
Drake, W. Raymond
Druffel, Ann

E
Eberhart, George
Ecker, Don
Edwards, Frank
Elders, Brit
Escamilla, Jose
Evers, Chris

F
Fawcett, George
Fawcett, Lawrence
Feindt, Carl
Filer, George
Firmage, Joseph
Fisher, Rick
Foltz, Chuck
Forgione Adriano
Foster, John
Fournet, Dewey
Fowler, Raymond E.
Fraknoi, Andrew
Freer, Neil
Friedman, Stanton
Fry, Daniel W.

G
Gardner, Martin
Gardiner, Philip
Geerts, L.C.

Geller, Uri
Gertz, John
Gevaerd, A. J.
Gilliland, James
Gitt, Werner
Glasgow, Dane
Goldberg, Bruce
Goldin, Dan
Good, Timothy
Goudie, Dale
Gordon, Stan
Green, Christopher
Green, Gabriel
Greenewald, John Jr.
Greenwood, Barry
Greer, Dr. Steven
Greer, Steven M.
Greywolf Leigh, Jason
Grissom, Gus,
Gross, Loren
Guerin, Michelle
Guerin, Pierre
Gunderson. Ted

H

Haines Richard F.
Haisch, Bernard Haley, Leah
Hall, Michael David
Hall, Brian.
Halt, Lt. Colonel Charles
Hamel, David
Hamilton, Bonnie Jean
Hamilton, Bill
Hamilton, Pamela
Han-Adam, Prince
Hancock, Graham
Hansen, Terry

Hansworth, Ross
Harder, James
Hare Tietze, Donna
Harris, Daniel
Harris Leopizzi, Paola
Harrison, Albert A.
Hartranft, J. B. Jr.
Harwit Amrani, Estelle Nora
Hayakawa, Norio
Hayes, Anna
Hennessey, Andrew
Heseltine, Gary
Hesemann, Michael
Hewes, Hayden
Hill, Betty and Barney
Hill, Paul R.
Hoagland, Richard C.
Holt, Lyssa Royal
Hopkins, Budd
Horne, Tom
Horowitz, Len
Horton, John W.
Houck, Jack
Howard, Chard.
Huneeus, J. Antonio
Hurtak, Desire
Hurtak, J.J.
Huyghe, Patrick
Hyman, Ray
Hynek J. Allen

I
Icke, David

J
Jacobs, Dr. David
Jamaludin, Ahmad
James, Tony
James, Larry

Johnson, Donald
Johnston, Miesha
Johnston, Colleen Jordan-Kauble, Debbie
Jung, Carl

K

Kaeser, Steven
Kasher, John C. "Jack"
Kasten, Len
Kean, Leslie
Keel, John A.
Keith, Jim
Kelleher, Colm A.
Ketchum Jessup, Morris
Randle, Kevin
Keyhoe, Donald E.
Kimball, Paul
Kitei, Dr. Lynne
Kirkwood, Guy
Klarer, Elizabeth
Klass Philip J.
Knapp, George
Koppang, Randy
Korff, Kal
Krapf, Phillip
Kurtz, Paul

L

Lake, Gina
Lake, Roy
Lamb, Barbara
Lambremont Webre, Alfred
Lazar, Bob
Lear, William
Lear, John
Ledger, Don
Leir, Roger

Leopizzi Harris, Paola
Leslie, Melinda
Lewels Joe
Lewis, Clyde
Li, Sun Shi
Liddle, David
Lindemann, Michael
Lloyd, Ellen
Loder, Ted
Lorenzen, Coral
Lorenzen, Jim
Lorgen, Eve
Lucas, George
Luukanen Kilde, Rauni-Leena

M

Maccabee, Dr. Bruce S.
Mack, Dr. John E.
Malin, Michael
Mantle, Philip
Marcel, Jesse, Jr.
Marcel, Jesse, Sr.
Marciniak, Barbara
Marrs, Jim
Maussan, Jaime
Maxwell, Jordan
McCampbell, James
McCannon, Tricia
McClendon, Sarah
McDonald, James Edward
McGonagle, Joe
Mead, Margaret
Meier, Billy
Melaris, Spyros
Menger, Howard
Menzel, Donald Howard
Mikhailovich Uvarov, Valery
Miller, Stuart
Mitchell, Edgar

Mitchell, Edgar
Montalk, Tom
Moon, Peter
Moore, Bill
Morehouse, David
Morse, Melvin
Moseley, Jim
Moulton Howe, Linda
Mourning, Steven
Myers III, Royce J.

N
Nance, Steve
Nichols, Preston
Nidle, Sheldon
Noori, George

O
O'Brien,Cathy
Ocean, Joan
O'Leary, Brian
Oberg, James
Oechsler, Bob
Oliphant, Ted
Oram, Mike
Orfeo, Angelucci

P
Pacaccini, Vitorio
Page, Eddie
Palmer Hoyt, Diana
Pandolfi, Ronald
Papadopoulos, Greg
Penninston, Sergeant Jim
Perala, Robert
Perkins, David
Pflock, Karl

Phillips, Mark
Phillips Ted
Pierson, Thomas
Poher, Claude
Pope, Nick
Popovich, Marina
Pratt, Bob
Pratt, David
Pursglove, David
Puthoff, Harold

R

Rael
Raith, Robert
Randall, Karen
Randle, Kevin
Randles, Jenny
Rashed, Sanad
Rawlings Gary
Redfern, Nick
Reed, Jonathan
Rense, Jeff
Rice, Boyd
Richardson, Geoff
Ridge Francis L.
Rixey More, John
Rob, Simone
Robbins, Peter
Roberts, Andy J.
Roberts, Brenda
Rockefeller, Laurance
Rockwell, Theodore
Rodwell, Mary
Roddenberry, Gene
Romanek, Stan
Rueckert, Carla
Ruppelt, Edward J.
Rutkowski, Chris

Rutledge, Harley

S
Sagan, Dr. Carl
Salas, Robert
Salla, Dr. Michael
Santilli, Ray
Sarfatti, Jack
Sauder, Richard
Scallion, Gordon-Michael
Schafer, Marcia
Schlemmer, Phyllis
Schloemp, Claudia
Schmitt, Donald R.
Schneider, Phil
Schratt, Michael
Schrodter, Willy
Schuessler, John
Scott, Jones
Semerov, Vladimir
Shandera, Jaime
Shapiro, Robert
Shargel, Lee
Shatner, William
Sheehan, Daniel
Shermer, Michael
Shi-Li, Sun
Shoemaker, David
Shostak, Seth
Simondini, Silvia
Sims, Derrel
Sitchin, Zecharia
Smith, Joseph
Smith, Yvonne
Smith, Dan
Smith, Wilbert B.
Smith, Yvonne
Sokolov, Michael

Sparks, Jim
Spencer, John L.
Spielberg, Steven
Sprinkle, Leo, R.
Stacy, Dennis
Stanford, Amitakh
Stanford, Ray
Stearns, Erik
Stevens, Wendelle
Stone, Clifford
Stonebrooke, Pamela
Stonehill, Paul
Story Macer, Eugenia
Story, Ronald
Strieber, Whitley
Stringfield, Leonard
Stuart, Miller
Stubblebine, Al
Sturrock, Peter A.
Summers, Marshall V.
Svahn, Clas
Swerdlow, Stewart
Swords, Michael

T

Talbot, Michael
Talbott, Nancy
Targ, Russell
Tarter, Jill
Taylor, Brice
Tellinger, Michael
Tesla, Nikola
Theofanous, Tom
Thomas, Andy
Thomas, William
Thomas, Kenn
Thuney, Matthew

Timmerman, John
Tito, Dennis
Tombaugh, Clyde
Truzzi, Marcello
Turnbull, Jed
Turner, Karla
Twyman, Tracey

V

Valerian, Val (John Grace)
Vallee, Dr. Jacques
Van Bebber, Mark
Van Flandern, Tom
Van Tassel, George
Vance, Davis
Vasquez, John
Velasco, Jean-Jacques
Velez, John
Vike, Brian
von Däniken, Erich

W

Wakely, Chuck
Waldrop, Don
Walt, Andrus
Walters, Ed
Walton, Travis
Ware, Donald M.
Warren, Lary
Waters, Mel
Watson, Nigel
Webb, Don
Welch, William
Webre Lambremont, Alfred
Whinnery Jim
White, Bob

Whitecliff, Angelika
Whitley, Strieber
Wilcock, David
Willes, Jeff
William, Hamilton
William, Lyne
Wilson, Katharina
Wilson, Robert Anton
Wilson, Steve
Winters, Randolph
Wolf, Michael
Wood, Robert. M.
Wood, Ryan S.
Woodward, Joan
Wright, Bruce

Y
Young, Kenny
Yurdozu, Farah

Y
Zerpa, Fabio
See Ufology

Autopsy of an aliens' dead body: During an "aliens' autopsy",
none of the operating surgeons and nurses inside the autopsy
room could stand the smell. They ran away "like a mad dog" said
one of the military nurses.
In fact, the odor was so strong, it invaded the whole compound.
They had to seal the room for 24 hours. Physicians at Walter Reed
Army Medical Center, became very concerned and alarmed, for
they sought that the smell could be very toxic.
Note: Worth mentioning here that no autopsy report from Walter
Reed was ever issued by a physician (Pathologist) who conducted
any kind of autopsy on dead aliens.

215

Instead, scattered and reconstructed medical notes (Unsigned) were sent to the Pentagon two days later.

This is not a normal military or medical procedure as any one might guess. But it did happen intentionally, and I am unable to elaborate further on this situation.

The names of the pathologists and assisting nurses were never revealed to "outsider-civilians".

And the preliminary notes vanished from the face of the earth. Thus, there is no way to honestly and accurately document the autopsy.

And most certainly, the autopsy was not filmed.

I am absolutely certain that no civilian or any officer below the rank of Colonel had access to any autopsy report. Even at the Pentagon, only two generals and one military surgeon had access to a medical report describing in details the anatomy and physiology of the aliens. Said report was then submitted to The White House.

To the best of my knowledge, there is only one original report which remained hidden somewhere in a secret military dossier at The Pentagon, and one copy of the report which was read by the President and YES disposed of. Grosso modo, and quite honestly, we don't know a thing about the aliens' autopsy. Yes, it did happen, but there are no records to substantiate the fact that it did happen.

Following the crash of an alien spaceship, indexed as Category AC1 (A=Alien; C=Craft; 1=Type 1), an autopsy was conducted on a dead alien body at Walter Reed Hospital (Walter Reed Army Medical Center, Washington, DC/Maryland).

And what the pathologists found astonished us immensely.

We did not know how to adequately and scientifically describe the internal organs of the aliens, how they functioned and what gave "a motion" to the alien's body.

The liquid that emerged from the alien's "glands" during the autopsy was of a green color and had an intoxicating odor. At first, we thought it was blood.

But surprisingly, it did not coagulate after it has been exposed to the air, as usually it happens with human blood. The pathologists became very confused, and consequently, more physicians were brought in to assess the situation. Still, no progress was made.

216

This confusion intensified, once the pathologists discovered that:
- 1-The alien had no glands,
- 2-The alien had no retina,
- 3-The alien had no genital organs,
- 4-The alien's so-called blood (Green liquid) had no cells, as it is the case with human blood which contains three types of cells:

a-Leukocytes (white blood cells),
b-Erythrocytes (red blood cells),
c-Thrombocytes (platelets)

Thus, to understand these anomalies, we needed more and more physicians who specialized in different medical areas/practices.
Consequently, more specialists were added to the roster.
And their names were never revealed to outsiders.
However, the number of physicians began to decrease by the mid of 1949, partially because the aliens began to explain to us how:
- 1-Their body functions,
- 2-What was that green liquid we thought it was blood,
- 3-How the tissues react to pulses,
- 4-Why didn't they have muscles, cells, blood, and genital organs,
- 5-How they reproduce.

By December of 1949, only one surgeon remained on the list of the attendees. And by the mid of 1950, no further medical staff was deemed necessary by the military. However two registered nurses were called upon from time to time.
Later on, the Lt. Nurse was transferred to West Germany, and the other one to Walter Reed.

Conspiracy theorists and ill-informed ufologists claimed that a nurse who allegedly attended an autopsy on a military base nearby Roswell vanished from the face of the earth, because the military got rid of her. This claim is false! The Lt. Nurse reached the rank of a major and was honorably discharged at age 49. The other nurse retired from the army at age 42, and died at age 81, somewhere in England. And none of them revealed any pertinent information about any kind of alien autopsy...to a certain degree.

217

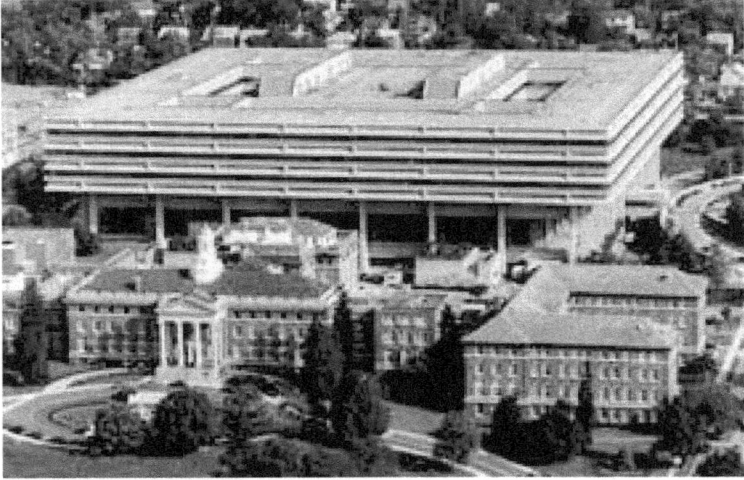

The Walter Reed Army Medical Center (WRAMC), where the aliens' autopsy was conducted in 1947. Walter Reed is about six miles from the Pentagon. Walter Reed Army Medical Center is located in Northern Washington, D.C. at 6900 Georgia Avenue NW, Washington DC 20307, between Rock Creek Park and Georgia Avenue near the Maryland-District of Columbia boundary.

Aviary: Name attributed by some colorful ufologists to alleged twelve whistle-blowers who have claimed that the United States government is in contact with Grays-aliens.

Avikhal "Abi-Khal": Name or title of the patriarch of an Anunnaki's family, and or a generation. From this Anunnaki's word, derived the Hebrew "Avi-khol", and the Arabic "Abi 'koul", which mean father of all. The Hebrew "Avi" and the Arabic "Abi" mean father. The Hebrew "khol", and the Arabic "Koul" mean all, or of all.

AVRO: AVRO Aircraft Canada was a Canadian aircraft company know for innovative designs. On February 11, 1953, The Toronto Star reported that a new kind of flying saucers has been developed at AVRO-Canada plant in Malton, Ontario, Canada.

And on February 16, Canada's Minister for Defense informed the Canadian House of Commons in Ottawa, that AVRO-Canada was developing a "mock-up" model od a flying saucer, capable of flying at 1,500 miles per hour.

However, in 1960 AVRO issued a statement confirming that AVRO flying saucer project has been terminated. More on this subject in Volume: Addendum.

AVRO flying saucer.

Aya: Sumerian/Akkadian. Noun.
Another name for the Anunnaki god Ea.
Aya and the Hebrew "Ehyeh asher ehyeh":
Scholars have identified a direct link of Yah (Yahweh) to the Mesopotamian and Anunnaki god Ea/Enki. They believe that Yahweh (Yahweh-Elohim) is a twist of the Akkadian-Sumerian god Ea/Enki, which is pronounced Ayya, or Aya.
The Hebrew "Ehyeh asher ehyeh" which means "I am that I am, tell them eyheh has sent you", Exodus 3:14, corresponds to Ea/Enki's declaration to Abraham when he told him, "I am who he is, your God."
The Hebrew word Ehyeh derived from the Sumero-Akkadian word Ayya, who was an Akkadian god.

219

And the Akkadian word Ayya derived from the Sumerian word Ea, and it was pronounced as Ay-a, and sometimes as Eh-ya, during the Ur III period, and the Sargonic's era.

"Ehyeh asher ehyeh" has no Hebraic origin:
According to the Hebrew texts and interpretation of Talmudic scholars, ehyeh asher ehyeh (I am that I am) was revealed by Yahweh to Moses at Mount Sinai. This is false because it is a fabricated speculation which appeared in a later period.
Phonetically and linguistically, it corresponds to the Babylonian Ea, Aya and Ayah, closely related to the Anunnaki god Enki. And Abraham and his father Terah being Arameans who lived in the Ur of the Chaldees in Lower Mesopotamia, have certainly heard of Ea and Aya, and consequently changed the words and their meaning to fit and serve their purposes.
The Tetragrammaton YHWH and Ehyeh have no Judaic-Hebraic origin. They appeared in Ugaritic, Byblian Phoenician, Syrian (Canaanite) and Moabite literature and texts written many years before the Jewish Bible was crafted, to name a few:
1-Ea's declaration to Abraham.
2-As "YW", which is an archaic Phoenician-Ugaritic divine name, which appeared in numerous texts and poems found in Ugarit, Tyre and Byblos, and especially in the poem of Baal-Hadad, and inscriptions found on an ancient Phoenician edifice in Byblos (Modern day Jbeil) around 1921. And the primordial meaning was "the passionate one."
Ehyeh asher ehyeh (I am that I am) is not the name of Yahweh, because its Phoenician epistemological origin is an attribute.
3-The Akkadian texts as "AWA-tu", which meant a person who reveals something important, in other words, a revealer.
4-As yahwa, and as yiha, which is the name of an ancient region in Egypt, mentioned in two passages from Rameses II-the text from Amara, Rameses III-the text from the Medinet Habu, and texts from Soleb, Amenhophis.
5-As the names of the Phoenician divinity E-Yu, also pronounced as Ieuh, Yeuh, Yah.
6-The Egyptian lists included a place called Y-h-wa, which historians, scholars and linguists identified with Seir.
In summary, the Jewish scholars and linguists failed to explain the epistemology and etymology of the Teragrammaton.

Even though, they were fully aware that their ancestors of the pre-Mosaic era used the digrammaton Ya, as an exclamation, and despite the fact that the early Canaanite-Hebrew names contained the prefix or suffix "Ya".

It is absolutely clear that in order to create their own "god", more precisely a new national Hebraic deity, they had to change "Ya" to Yahweh, and it was easily done, from Ugaritic, Phoenician, Proto-Palmyrian, ancient Aramaic and Nabatean, and Syriac to Hebrew. And to add credibility to this transition, they equated it with the Hebrew verb "Hayah".

Thus, "Yah-weh" and the verb "Hayah" (to be) were transmuted into a pseudo Hebrew etymology to offer us a new definition of the Teragrammaton: "The One Who causes to be", as well as "He Who brings things to pass." And it worked like a charm!!

Ayling: Name of the son of Elizabeth Klarer and her husband Akon, who is an extraterrestrial being from Meton, a planet of Proxima Centuri that, at a distance of about 4.3 light years, is our nearest stellar neighbor. Ayling lives on his planet Meton with his alien father, as claimed by Klarer, who wrote a fabulous book on the subject, titled "Beyond the Light Barrier".

*** *** ***

Published by

Times Square Press
New York, Berlin
Website: www.timessquarepress.com

Printed in the
United States of America and Germany
2014

www.ingramcontent.com/pod-product-compliance
Lightning Source LLC
Chambersburg PA
CBHW020609270326
41927CB00005B/252